THE BIG BOOK OF RECORDS

English edition translated from the Italian and edited by
Maureen Spurgeon

Brown Watson
ENGLAND

Original Italian text: Stefano Sibella
Illustrations: Davide Bonadonna

Italian Editor: Stefano Sibella
Editorial and Production Assistant: Tiziana Campana
Art Editor: Marco Volpati
Production: Studio ICG di Guglielmo Incerti Caselli
Production Editor: Roberto Ghidoli
Picture Researcher: Stefano Sibella

Photographic references: Archivo IGDA; NASA; M.Volpati

ISBN: 0-7097-1575-7

Il Grande Libro dei Record
© 2002 Istituto Geografico De Agostini S.p.A., Novara
© 2003 Brown Watson, English edition
Reprinted 2003

CONTENTS

WORLD RECORDS
THE
EARTH

The size of the world

The total area of the Earth is 510,250,000 square kilometres (sq. km.) The total area covered by **seas** is 360,650,000 sq. km. - plus 1,700,000 sq. km. covered by **lakes**, and almost 14,000,000 sq. km. covered by **ice**. This means that over two thirds of our planet (70%) is covered by water. Of the remaining surface, 35% (51,000,000 sq. km.) is covered by **mountains** and **mountainous areas**, 37% (53,000,000 sq. km.) **hilly areas** and about 28% (46,000,000 sq. km.) **plains** (level ground). The areas of seas and land are not equally distributed between the two hemispheres of the globe. In the northern hemisphere the land surface takes up 39% of the total area and the seas 61%. In the southern hemisphere only 16% is land area, the remaining 84% is covered by water.

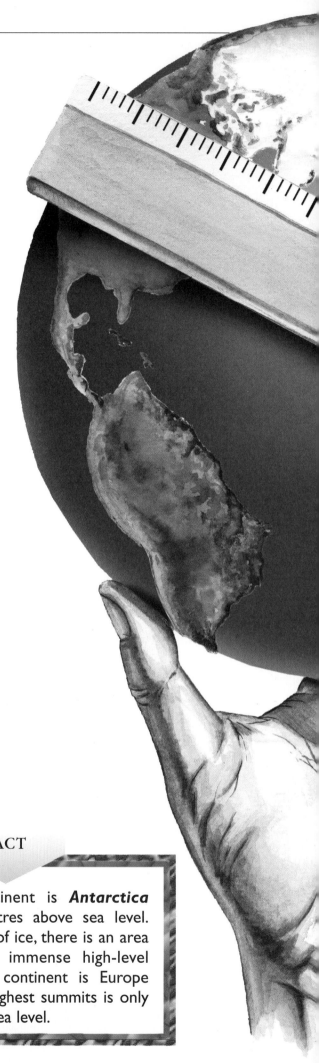

Man with globe
Painting by the 17th century Spanish artist
Diego Velásquez

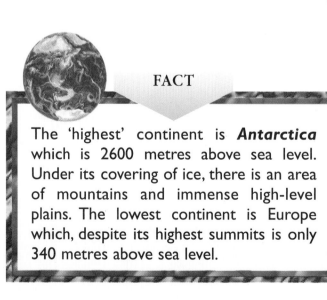

FACT

The 'highest' continent is **Antarctica** which is 2600 metres above sea level. Under its covering of ice, there is an area of mountains and immense high-level plains. The lowest continent is Europe which, despite its highest summits is only 340 metres above sea level.

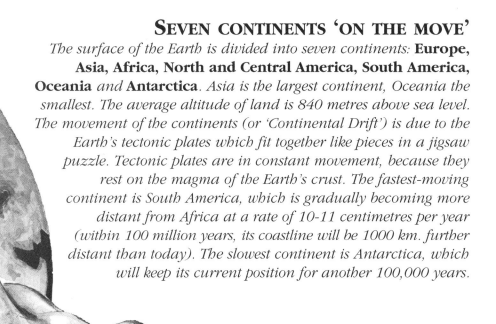

SEVEN CONTINENTS 'ON THE MOVE'

The surface of the Earth is divided into seven continents: **Europe, Asia, Africa, North and Central America, South America, Oceania** *and* **Antarctica**. *Asia is the largest continent, Oceania the smallest. The average altitude of land is 840 metres above sea level. The movement of the continents (or 'Continental Drift') is due to the Earth's tectonic plates which fit together like pieces in a jigsaw puzzle. Tectonic plates are in constant movement, because they rest on the magma of the Earth's crust. The fastest-moving continent is South America, which is gradually becoming more distant from Africa at a rate of 10-11 centimetres per year (within 100 million years, its coastline will be 1000 km. further distant than today). The slowest continent is Antarctica, which will keep its current position for another 100,000 years.*

Two pictures by the 17th century Dutch artist Jan Vermeer: below, the Geographer; to the left, a detail of the painting The Astronomer.

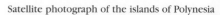
Satellite photograph of the islands of Polynesia

▶ Measurements of the Earth

The circumference of the Earth is 40,076 km. This is measured at the **equator**, the imaginary line which divides our planet in two hemispheres, the southern and the northern. Here, at the equator, the Earth spins at a constant speed of 100 km. per hour, yet it takes more than two weeks to complete a full spin, because the equator is so vast. The volume (mass) of the Earth is 1,083,319,780,000 km.

The Indian Ocean and the coast of Madagascar

The Polynesian island of Bora-Bora

The Pacific Ocean washes the Australian coast

FACT

Most of the water on Earth (97.3%) is salt. Less than 3% is fresh water, and approximately two thirds of this is trapped in the ice of the North and South Poles. About 1.1% fresh water flows in rivers, lakes, springs or through canals.

Port on the Black Sea in Turkey

HOW DEEP IS THE SEA...

The largest ocean is the **Pacific***, which covers a surface of 179,650,000 sq. km. - one third of the entire planet, followed by the* **Atlantic Ocean***, 106,100,000 sq. km. and the* **Indian Ocean***, 74,900,000 sq. km. The smallest ocean is the* **Arctic Glacier***, which at 14,060,000 sq. km., is six times larger than the* **Mediterranean Sea***. At the interior of each ocean, geographers have identified 36 particular zones as seas. The most extensive sea is the* **South China Sea** *with a surface area of 3,447,000 sq. km. The smallest is the* **Black Sea***, an inland sea between Europe and Asia with a surface area of 413,000 sq. km. At least 25,000* **islands***, more than all the other islands in the world put together, are in the waters of the Pacific Ocean. This is also the world's deepest ocean, with an average depth of over 3000 metres below surface level. It is in the Pacific Ocean we find the* **geographic point** *furthest from any coast - 2575 km.*

A view of the Ross Sea, Antarctica

From the Malayan peninsular to Panama, an expanse of water over 24,000 km. covers a third of the Earth's surface - the Pacific Ocean

The ice cap of Antarctica

Down in the depths

The deepest ocean trench in the world is the **Marianna Trench** in the Pacific Ocean, 11,022 metres below the surface of the sea - seven times deeper than the Grand Canyon in Arizona, USA. A ball of lead weighing one kilogram thrown into the water would take at least one hour to reach the sea-bed. The **Puerto Rico Trench** at 9212 metres is the deepest point in the Atlantic Ocean. The highest tides in the world have been recorded in Canada, at the **Bay of Fundy** where the difference of level between low and high water is over 15 metres.

The icy coastline of Antarctica

Low tide at the Bay of Fundy

Satellite photograph of Greenland

ISLANDS...

*Islands occupy 7.2% of the Earth's surface - that is, around 10,800,000 sq. km. Apart from Australia, often regarded as a continent in itself, the largest island in the world is **Greenland** which is 2,175,000 sq. km. in area, ten times the size of **Britain**. 85% of Greenland's territory is only 800 km. distant from the North Pole, and is covered with ice, which varies in thickness from a minimum of 1.5 metres to a maximum of 3 metres. The length of Greenland's coast, 39,627 km., almost equals the circumference of the Earth at the equator, whilst the distance from north to south is just over 2670 km., more than the width of the Sahara Desert. It is more extensive than both Spain and Portugal put together. Next largest island is **New Guinea**, 808,572 sq. km. in area, then **Borneo**, 751,000 sq. km.*

FACT

Ocean currents are like great rivers which flow in the depths of the oceans; the gigantic **Antarctic Circumpolar Current** goes all around the Earth! The *abyssal plains* are immense underwater plains which extend for hundreds of kilometres at a depth of up to 6000 metres.

Very small marine creatures swarm among the depths of the sea. Seen close-up, they look like something out of a nightmare!

Tongues of ice

The largest expanse of ice in the world is the **Lambert Glacier** in Antarctica. It is at least 64 km. wide and extends for 402 km. Next largest is the **Hubbard Glacier** in Alaska, 106 km. long. The fastest-moving glacier is also in Alaska. This is the **Columbia Glacier** which moves on average 20 metres each day. Alpine (mountain) glaciers advance on average about 50 metres in a year.

The **Antarctic Ice Cap** is so vast that it would be able to cover almost all North America. Its minimum thickness is 1.3 km. If it were to melt, the level of the sea would rise by 60 metres.

Oceania is the only continent where there are no glaciers.

Glaciers in Alaska

Alpine glacier

Iceberg in the icy seas of the Arctic

The Grand Canyon of Arizona

Due to the action of the winds and the seas, rocks of ice up to 20 metres in height protrude from the polar ice pack.

FACT

The deepest gorge in the world is the **Grand Canyon** in Arizona, USA. It is 350 km. long and 1600 metres deep, gorged out of the Earth during the course of billions of years by the Colorado River.

Archipelago

An *archipelago* is a group of islands. The largest is the **Indonesian Archipelago**. This consists of more than 15,000 islands, with a combined surface of at least 1,919,317 sq. km.

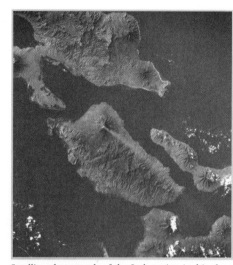

Satellite photograph of the Indonesian Archipelago

Norwegian fjord

Fjords

The **North-West Fjord** in Southern Greenland is the longest in the world. It indents inland for 313 km.

13

Always higher!

The whole of the mountain chain which rises up from the depth of the oceans, the **Mid-Oceanic Ridge**, forms an uninterrupted long chain of 65,000 km., with peaks up to 4200 metres.
The most imposing mountain chain on Earth is the **Karakorum Range of the Himalayas**. Of its 109 mountains, 96 are higher than 7300 metres and ten of those peaks are higher than 8000 metres!
The longest mountain chain in the world is the **Andes Cordillera** which crosses through South America for 7600 km. - seven times more extensive than the Alps.
On the border of Nepal and Tibet in the Himalayas is **Mount Everest**, 8,850 high and the highest mountain in the world. Second highest is **K2** (sometimes called Mount Godwin-Austen), 8611 metres in height and which is part of the Karakorum Mountain Chain.

FACT

Even though it is half submerged in the waters of the Pacific Ocean, the **Mauna Kea**, an ancient dormant volcano in Hawaii, is higher even than Everest, at 9754 metres.
Vinson Massif is the highest peak in the Antarctic, with a height of 5140 metres.

The mountain chain of Karakoram

The volcano Kilauea, Hawaii

At the top of the world

Mount Everest was conquered for the first time in 1953 by *Edmund Hillary* (photograph, left) a New Zealand mountaineer, and Nepalese Sherpa *Tenzing Norgay* (below, shown with Hillary at the base camp) after climbing all 8848 metres. Italian mountaineer *Reinhold Messner* in 1980 became the first person to climb Everest solo. He also holds the record for climbing all 14 of the world's highest mountains which exceed a height of 8000 metres, and without using oxygen cylinders.

Mount Everest in The Himalayas

The Andes Cordillera

Mirrors of water

The **Caspian Sea** in Asia, with a surface area of 371,000 sq. km. and 1225 km. long is the largest saltwater lake in the world.

Lake Superior, one of the Great Lakes between the United States and Canada, is the largest freshwater lake - 83,131 sq. km.

Lake Baikal in Siberia, Russia, is the deepest, with a depth of just over 1500 metres - four times deeper than Lake Superior and with enough water to quench the thirst of the total population of our planet for at least half a century. It is also the oldest lake in the world, with an age estimated at 30 million years!

Lake Titicata in Peru, with a surface area of 8300 sq. km. and 3810 metres above sea level is the highest navigable lake (a lake through which ships can pass) in the world.

Lake Tanganyika in Africa is the longest in the world at 660 km. and with a depth of up to 1470 metres.

The size of a lake has no bearing at all on its depth. For instance, **Lake Como** in Northern Italy is very small, but has a maximum depth of 410 metres. **Lake Chad** in Nigeria (see below) is 100 times larger, but nowhere does it exceed a depth of 12 metres, and mostly the depth is only 1.5 metres!

Finland is the country with the most lakes - over 55,000!

View of Lake Titicata

View of Lake Chad

GULFS

*The largest **gulf** in the world is the **Bay of Bengal** in Asia, which has a maximum depth of 5258 metres and a surface area of 2,172,000 sq. km., almost as large as the Mediterranean Sea.*

*Second largest is the **Gulf of Mexico** which receives waters from one of the longest rivers in the world, the Mississippi-Missouri and covers a surface of 1,544,000 sq. km.*

The 16,000 sq. km. surface of Lake Chad is reduced by at least one tenth every ten years. This is due to the surrounding land becoming desert.

FACT

Lake Vostok in Antarctica buried beneath 4000 metres of ice, is the oldest on Earth, hidden from the rest of the world for at least half a million years. It is 100 metres deep and has a surface area of 14,000 sq. km.

View of the Caspian Sea

View of Lake Baikal

Great swamps

The **Everglades** are known as the great swamps of Florida, USA. In fact, it is all a vast expanse of marshland, the result of an immense river of water which pours out from the Atlantic Ocean. The Everglades cover an area 80 km. wide, 106 km. long, but only 15 centimetres deep.

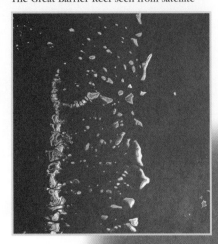

The Great Barrier Reef seen from satellite

Volcanoes

On Earth there are about one thousand active volcanoes. There are many others which are inactive or 'dormant', such as **Mount Fuji** in Japan and **Mauna Kea**, in Hawaii. **Mauna Loa** in the Hawaiin Archipelago is the largest active volcano in the world - 4170 metres high and 9144 metres up from the sea bed. **Llullaillaco** on the borders of Chile and Argentina reaches up to the sky at a height of 6723 metres, more than 20 times the height of the Eiffel Tower!

Mount Fuji

View of the Everglades

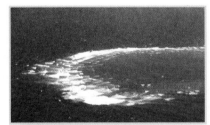

The Great Barrier Reef

Coral reefs

The longest coral reef in the world is the **Great Barrier Reef** which extends for more than 2000 km., along the North-East coast of Australia. It is so large that astronauts were able to identify it from space.

A sperm whale resting in the depths of a coral atoll - a ring-shaped island originating from the summit of an ancient underwater volcano.

The Turfan Depression   View of the Dead Sea

Lowest places.

Between Israel and Jordan is the lowest point on Earth, the **Dead Sea**. Its banks are 400 metres below sea level. Compared to this, the **Turfan Depression**, a mountain basin in China is quite 'high up' - only 154 metres below sea level.

FACT

The most extensive plain in the world is the **Western Siberian Plain** in Russia, with a surface area of 2,250,000 sq. km. - 50 times larger than the **Padana Plain**, Northern Italy. Compared to this the **Argentinian Pampas** takes up the relatively small area of 1,250,000 sq. km.

Deserts

An estimated 5% of the surface of the Earth is covered by desert.

The largest desert in the world is the *Sahara Desert* in North Africa which extends over 9,100,000 sq. km. an area almost equal to that of the United States and larger than all the other 12 major deserts of the world put together.

The second largest is the *Australian Desert*, 3.6 million sq. km., the third largest is the *Arabian Desert*, 1.3 million sq. km., and then there is the *Gobi Desert* in Asia, one million sq. km. The *Sonoran Desert* in Arizona is the largest desert in North America - 310,000 sq. km.

The Australian Desert

The Gobi Desert

The Sonoran Desert

FACT

The *Rub'Al Khali* in Saudi Arabia is the largest sandy desert in the world, an expanse of sand hills or 'dunes' up to 100 metres high. At 2,300,000 sq. km. it is as large as France. But, because of the hot climate, there are no villages and only groups of nomads live there.

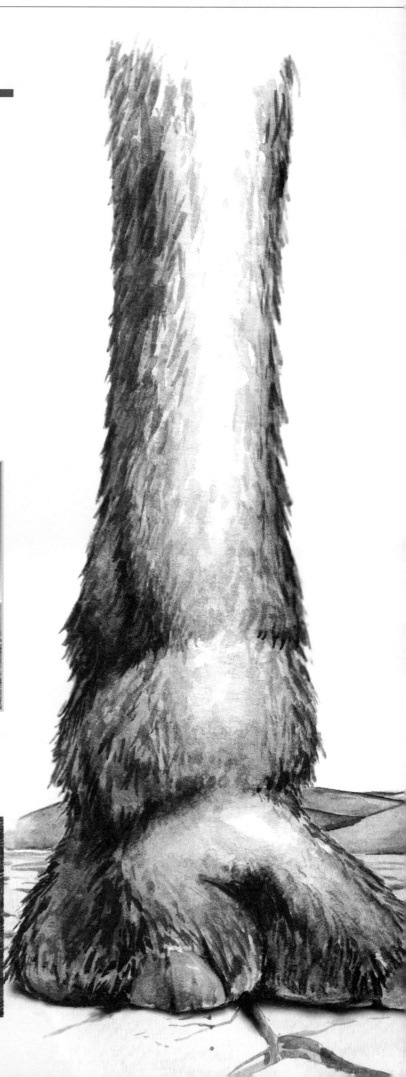

MOVING SAND DUNES

Within the huge **Western Erg**, an area of the Sahara as large as Austria, enormous crescent moon-shaped dunes form. These 'sand boats' suddenly appear across the desert, being blown by the wind, and moving up to 30 metres in one year. They are seen as the spirits of the desert by the Tuareg, the people of the Sahara. Great walls of sand can rise up to 1500 metres from the ground, making barriers up to 500 km. thick. The howling wind can reach speeds of 50 km. an hour, blotting out every sound, and sometimes even day-time sunlight. Then the grains of sand catch the breath, penetrating into every crack. Sometimes the sand can even reach Europe, as in 1947, when the Swiss Alps were tinged red by Algerian sand.

Only the dromedary can venture across the sands of the desert without sinking into the sand, travelling for days on end.

A Tuareg in the Sahara

Old deserts

The *Namib Desert* is the oldest in the world, as well as being the driest desert in Africa. It extends over 2080 km. from Angola to Namibia, and its width varies from 10 to 160 km. To the north there is a mixture of rock and gravel. To the south is the River Kuiseb, with an enormous sand dune shaped by the wind and arranged in straight rows, like so many mountain chains of sand sculptures. Here, the largest deposits of diamonds in the world have been found.

The Namib Desert

A sand dune in the Ténéré Region of the Sahara Desert, Niger

Rivers

The longest river in the world is the **Nile** which flows for 6671 km. Second longest is the **Amazon**. This is 6280 km. long, but it transports more water than the Nile. Each day the Amazon pours back into the Atlantic Ocean a quantity of water sufficient to supply the houses of all the people in the United States for at least five months - in fact, 20% of all the fresh water which flows naturally into the oceans of the world. By contrast, the Nile carries 200 times less water than the Amazon. Among the world's largest rivers, the **Mississippi-Missouri** with a length of 6021 km. and the **Yangtze** river which flows through China for 5987 km. are high on the list.

At least 5000 cubic metres of water per second tumble down from the world's largest waterfalls

The course of the Mississippi

The Nile within sight of the Aswan Dam

The River Amazon

Waterfalls

Angel Falls in Venezuela, South America, is the highest waterfall in the world - at 972 metres, this is 15 times higher than the *Niagara Falls* on the borders of the United States and Canada. Although the Niagara Falls is wider by almost 1 km. its 60 metres 'drop' is shorter. So, the Niagara Falls is also beaten by the 108 metre 'drop' of the *Victoria Falls* on the borders of Zambia and Zimbabwe in Africa. Here, the enormous volume of water which pours from this waterfall makes a deafening noise and produces a cloud of vapour visible at over 30 km. distance. The record for width - 10.7 km. - is held by the *Khone Falls*, in Laos. The *Boyoma Falls* in Zaire, is the waterfall which transports the greatest amount of water - 17,000 cubic metres per second.

Niagara Falls

Angel Falls

Victoria Falls

Grottos and rocks

Ayers Rock

The **Mammoth Cave** in the United States is the longest network of caves in the world - 560 km. The **Réseau Jean Bernard** in France is the deepest grotto so far discovered with a depth of 1535 metres.

The **Lubang Nasib Bagus** in Malaysia is the largest cave chamber on Earth. At 700 metres long, 450 metres wide and 150 metres high, it makes a 'room' large enough to contain up to eight Jumbo Jet aircraft.

The world's longest underwater cavern is the **Sistema Ox Bel Ha** in Mexico. It extends for over 70 km.

The longest **stalagtite** hangs down 60 metres from the roof of the **Cueva de Nerja** in Spain, whilst the highest **stalagmite** rises 32 metres from the ground of the **Krasnohorska** grotto in the Czech Republic.

Among the world's strangest rock formations - in Turkey, in the region of **Cappadocia** there extends a fairy-tale walkway, made up of fantastic spires of rock up to 30 metres high, called 'the fairy path' by the local people. Equally famous are the **Fairy Towers of Ürgüp**, curious volcanic rock formations, moulded by rain and the eroded by the wind. During the course of more than 2000 years, people have transformed these rocks into homes and places of worship.

Along the northern coast of Northern Ireland is a spectacular row of at least 40,000 basalt columns, ranging in height from 6 to 12 metres and extending over 300 metres of cliff. This is called the **Giant's Causeway** and it began to form about ten centuries ago. A flow of lava from a volcano cooled down very slowly. As this happened, the weather and the atmosphere gradually 'moulded' the flow into the form of enormous organ pipes, partly buried beneath the earth of County Antrim. According to Irish legend, this causeway was once a road for giants to travel across the Irish Sea to Scotland.

'Fairy Towers' of Ürgüp

The 'organ pipes' of the Giant's Causeway, Northern Ireland

Strange rock formation in the Grand Canyon

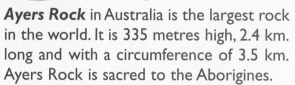
The legendary Giant's Causeway seen from above

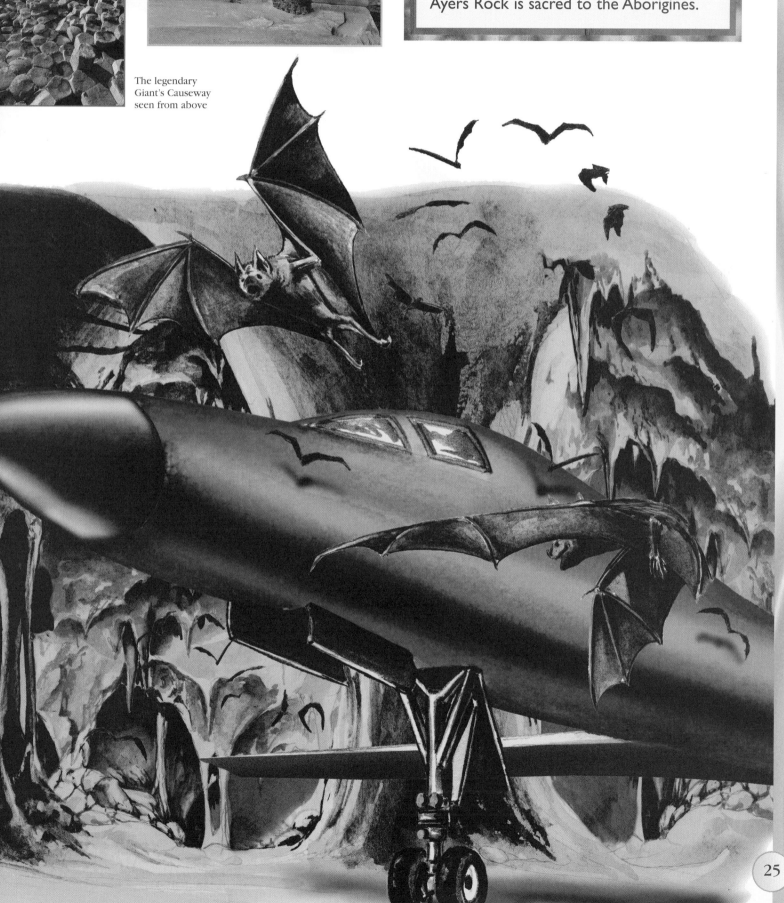

Hot and cold...

The lowest temperatures on Earth, between 40°C and 50°C below zero, have been recorded in the **Antarctic**. The lowest temperature ever recorded was at **Vostok** in 1983 - 89.6°C below zero. The South Pole is also the windiest place on Earth. At **Commonwealth Bay**, gusts can reach a speed of 320 km. per hour. The village of **Oymyakon** in **Siberia** is probably the coldest inhabited place in the world - in 1933, a temperature of 68°C below zero was recorded. **Death Valley** in California is probably the hottest place on Earth. Here, for almost two months of the year, the temperature hovers around 50°C. The hottest temperature ever recorded of 57.7°C was at **El Azizia** in Libya.

The Atacama Desert

Death Valley, California

Rain, rain...

In the zone of **Shillong** (see picture) in India, rainfall can reach 12,000 millimetres per year. Most of the rain falls during the months between June and September. The locality of **Buenaventura** in Columbia is lashed by heavy rain - almost 7000 millimetres of water per year - which floods fields and homes.
By contrast, the **Atacama Desert** in Chile is the driest place in the world. The drought is such that this registers only one or two falls of rain in one century.

View of the Antarctic, one of the coldest places on Earth

SNOW...

In the course of one fall of snow lasting just a few hours, millions and millions of snowflakes swirl in the air, each flake quite different to any other. The deepest and heaviest **snowfall** ever recorded was on New Year's Eve 1971 to 1972 on Paradise, Mount Rainier in the State of Washington, United States. 31,102mm of snow fell, resulting in a covering of snow over 30 metres high.

FACT

The heaviest *hailstone* ever recorded fell in Bangladesh in 1986.

27

Records - the continents

Europe

Surface area:	10,369,644 sq. km.
Population:	702,000,000 inhabitants
Largest country:	Russia (European part) 4,238,500 sq. km.
Smallest country in the world:	Vatican City, 0.44 sq. km.
Most heavily-populated country:	Russia (European part) 113,657,000 inhabitants
Least populated country:	Vatican City, 1000 inhabitants
Most heavily-populated city:	Paris, 9,318,821 inhabitants
Length of coastline:	37,900 km.
Longest peninsula:	Scandinavia, 800,000 sq. km.
Longest mountain chain:	Carpathians, 1300 km.
Highest mountain:	Mont Blanc (France/Italy) 4807 metres
Largest island:	Britain, 229,885 sq. km.
Largest gulf (bay):	Gulf of Bothnia, 117,000 sq. km.
Longest fjord:	Sognefjord (Norway), 240 km.
Lowest place:	Volga Delta, 28 metres below sea level
Largest lake:	Ladoga (Russia) 18,400 sq. km.
Longest river:	Volga (Russia) 3531 km. surface area - 1,360,00 sq. km.
Largest active volcano:	Etna (Italy), 3323 m.
Highest waterfall:	Gavarnie (France) 421 km.
Highest capital city:	Andorra la Vella, 1070 m
Most southerly inhabited place:	Ny-Ålesund (Svalbard)
Highest density population worldwide:	Principality of Monaco, 16,923 inhabitants per sq. km.
Lowest density population:	Iceland, 3 inhabitants per sq. km.
Country with the youngest population:	Albania; 30% of people are less than 15 years old
Country with the oldest population in the world:	Italy and Greece; 48% of people are more than 60 years old
Country with the most men:	Andorra - 113 males for each 100 females
Country with the most women:	Lettonia - 83 males for each 100 females
Principal port:	Rotterdam (Netherlands)
Longest bridge:	Øresund (Denmark/Sweden) 7845 metres
Largest hydroelectric installation:	Volgograd (Russia) 2,563,000 kilowatts generated in one year.

Asia

Surface area:	44,661,151 sq. km.
Population:	3,640,693,000 inhabitants
Largest country:	Russia (Asiatic part) 12,836,900 sq. km.
Smallest country:	Maldives, 298 sq. km.
Most heavily-populated country in the world:	China - 1,248,100,000 inhabitants
Least populated country:	Maldives, 278,000 inhabitants
Most densely-populated city:	Chongqing (China) 30,600,000 inhabitants
Length of coastline:	69,900 km.
Longest peninsula in the world:	Arabian Peninsula, 2,730,000 sq. km.
Longest mountain chain:	Himalaya-Karakoram, 2500 km.
Highest mountain in the world:	Everest (Nepal/China) 8850 metres
Largest altopiano (high plain) in the world:	Tibet (China) 1,200,000 sq. km.
The highest pass in the world:	Karakoram Pass (Himalayas) 5575 metres
Largest desert:	Gobi, 1,096,000 sq. km.
Largest island:	New Guinea, 785,000 sq. km.
Largest gulf (bay) in the world:	Bay of Bengal, 2,172,000 sq. km.
Lowest place:	Dead Sea, Israel, 400 metres below sea level
Largest lake in the world:	Caspian Sea (Europe/Asia) 371,000 sq. km.
Deepest lake in the world:	Baikal (Russia), 1620 metres
Longest river:	Chang Jiang (Yellow River, China) 5800 km. long; surface area 1,826,715 sq. km.
Largest active volcano:	Kyluchevskoy, 4750 metres
Highest waterfall:	Gersoppa Falls, (India) 253 metres
Highest capital city:	Lhasa (Tibet) 3630 metres
Most northern inhabited place:	Ny-Ålesund, Svalbard Islands, Arctic Ocean
Highest density population:	Singapore, 5129 inhabitants per sq. km.
Lowest density population worldwide:	Mongolia, 1.6 inhabitants per sq. km.
Country with the youngest population:	Yemen; 48% of people are less than 15 years old
Country with the oldest population:	Japan; 45% of people are more than 60 years old
Country with the most men:	Qatar - 189 males for each 100 females
Country with the most women in the world:	Georgia - 92 males for each 100 females
Principal port:	Chiba (Japan)
Longest suspension bridge in the world:	Akashi Kaikyo (Japan) 3911 metres
Largest dam in the world:	Three Gorges Dam on the River Yangtze (China) 1045 sq. m
Highest tower in the world:	Petronas Towers, Kuala Lumpur, Malaysia, 452 metres
Largest airport in the world:	Chek Lap Kok (Hong Kong) 1248 hangars
Longest underwater railway tunnel in the world:	Seikan (Japan) 54 metres

▶ Records - the continents

Africa

Surface area:	30,210,372 sq. km.
Population:	763,621,000 inhabitants
Largest country:	Sudan, 503,890 sq. km.
Smallest country:	Seychelles, 455 sq. km.
Most heavily-populated country:	Nigeria, 108,945,000 inhabitants
Least populated country:	Seychelles, 77000 inhabitants
Most heavily-populated city:	Cairo, Egypt, 9,900,000 inhabitants
Length of coastline:	30,500 km.
Longest mountain chain:	Atlanta, 2400 km.
Highest mountain:	Kilimanjaro (Kenya/Tanzania) 5895 metres
Largest plain:	Serengeti, 14,760 sq. km.
Largest desert in the world:	Sahara, 9,000,000 sq. km.
Largest island:	Madagascar, 587,000 sq. km.
Lowest place:	Lake Assal (Djibouti), 150 metres below sea level
Largest lake:	Lake Victoria, 68, 100 sq. km.
Longest river in the world:	Nile, 6671 km. surface area 2,867,000 sq. km.
Largest active volcano:	Cameroon (Cameroon) 4070 m.
Highest waterfall:	Tugela (S. Africa) 948 metres
Highest capital city:	Addis Abeba (Ethiopia) 2408 m
Highest temperature recorded worldwide:	57.7°C at El Azizia (Libya)
Highest density population:	Mauritius, 617 inhabitants per sq. km.
Lowest density population:	Namibia, 2 inhabitants per sq. km.
Country with the youngest population in the world:	Uganda; 30% of people are less than 15 years old
Country with the oldest population :	Seychelles, 19% of inhabitants are more than 60 years old
Country with the most men:	Libya - 108 males for each 100 females
Country with the most women:	Cape Verde - 87 males for each 100 females
Principal port:	Casablanca (Morocco)
Largest hydroelectric installation:	Cahora Bassa (Mozambique) 4,150,00 kilowatts, generated in one year
Highest building:	Carlton Centre, Johannesburg, South Africa 220 metres
Highest railway:	Mombasa-Kampala, 2784 m
Longest canal in the world:	Suez Canal, 161 km.
Largest shipping line in the world:	Liberia, 59,800.742 tonnage

North and Central America

Surface area:	24,229,484 sq. km.
Population:	475,817,000 inhabitants
Largest country:	Canada, 9,970,610 sq. km.
Smallest country:	Saint Kitts and Nevis, 269 sq. km.
Most heavily-populated country:	USA, 276,218,000 inhabitants
Least populated country:	Saint Kitts and Nevis, 39,000 inhabitants
Most heavily-populated city:	New York, USA, 19,938,492 inhabitants
Longest mountain chain:	Rocky Mountains, USA, 4500 km.
Highest mountain:	Mount McKinley, USA 6194 metres
Largest island:	Greenland (Principality of Denmark) 2,175,600 sq. km.
Largest gulf:	Gulf of Mexico, 1,544,000 sq.km.
Lowest place:	Death Valley, 86 metres below sea level
Largest lake:	Lake Superior, USA, 84,131 sq. km.
Deepest lake:	Crater Lake, SW. Oregon, USA, 589 metres
Longest river:	Mississippi-Missouri, 5620 km. area surface 3,328,000 sq. km.
Largest active volcano:	Mauna Loa, Hawaii, USA, 4,170 sq. km. 9144 metres below sea level
Largest waterfall:	Yosemite, Eastern California, USA, 739 metres
Largest valley in the world:	Grand Canyon Arizona, USA: 446 km long; 16 km wide; 1600 metres deep
Longest frontier/border in the world:	Canada-USA, 6416 km
Highest geyser in the world:	Steamboat Geyser, Yellowstone, USA, 115 metres
Highest inhabited locality in the world:	Leadville, Colorado, USA, 3109 metres
Lowest inhabited locality in the world:	Calipatria, California, USA, 56 metres below sea level
Highest density population:	Barbados, 624 inhabitants per sq. km.
Lowest density population:	Canada, 3 inhabitants per sq. km.
Country with the youngest population:	Guatemala; 44% of people are less than 15 years old
Country with the oldest population:	Canada, 33% of inhabitants are more than 60 years old
Country with the most men:	Dominica - 108 males for each 100 females
Country with the most women:	Antigua and Barbuda - 92 males for each 100 females
Principal port:	Vancouver, Canada
Largest Theme Park in the world:	Disney World, USA, 122 sq. km.
Largest airport in the world:	O'Hare, Chicago, USA
Longest causeway bridge in the world:	Pontchartrain, Detroit, Louisiana, USA, 38,350 metres
Longest railway tunnel:	Cascade Range, Washington, USA, 12,550 metres

▶ Records - the continents

South America

Surface area:	17,857,561 sq. km.
Population:	337,812,000 inhabitants
Largest country:	Brazil, 8,547,393 sq. km.
Smallest country:	Trinidad and Tobago, 5128 sq. km.
Most heavily-populated country:	Brazil, 163,948,000 inhabitants
Least populated country:	Suriname, 415,000 inhabitants
Most heavily-populated city:	Sao Paolo, Brazil, 16,583,234 inhabitants
Length of coastline:	28,700 km.
Most extensive peninsular:	La Guaijra (Columbia/Venezuela) 14,000 sq. km.
Longest mountain chain in the world:	Andes Mountains, 7500 km.
Highest mountain:	Aconcagua, Chile/Argentina, 6959 metres
Largest plain:	The Pampas, Argentina/Paraguay, 1,250,000 sq. km.
Lowest place:	Penisula Valdés, Argentina, 40 m below sea level
Largest lake:	Maracaibo, Venezuela, 14,243 sq. km.
Longest river:	River Amazon, 6280 km. surface area 7,050,000 sq. km.
River with the largest amount of water:	River Amazon, 200,000 cu. m./sec.
Largest active volcano:	Lascar, Chile, 6,641 metres
Largest waterfall in the world:	Angel Falls, Venezuela, 972 metres
Largest lagoon in the world:	Lagoa dos Potos, Brazil, 9,850 sq. km.
Driest place in the world:	Atacama Desert, Chile
Highest capital city in the world:	La Páz, Bolivia, 3636 metres
Highest city:	Potosi, Bolivia, 3976 metres
Highest inhabited locality in the world:	Aucanquilcha, Chile, 5300 metres
Most southerly city in the world:	Ushuaia, Argentina
Highest density population:	Trinidad and Tobago, 251 inhabitants per sq. km.
Lowest density population:	Suriname, 2.5 inhabitants per sq. km.
Countries with the youngest population:	Bolivia and Paraguay, 40% of people are less than 15 years old
Country with the oldest population:	Uruguay, 34% of inhabitants are more than 60 years old
Country with the most men:	Ecuador - 101 males for each 100 females
Country with the most women:	Argentina - 96 males for each 100 females
Highest railway in the world:	Lima to La Oroya, Peru, 4829 metres
Largest hydroelectric installation:	Itaipù, Paraguay/Brazil, 13,320,000 kilowatts generated in one year

Oceania

Surface area:	8,522,559 sq. km.
Population:	31,469,000 inhabitants
Largest country:	Australia, 7,682,300 sq. km.
Smallest country:	Nauru, 21 sq. km.
Most heavily-populated country:	Australia, 18,962,000 inhabitants
Least populated countries:	Nauru and Tuvalu, 11,000 inhabitants
Most heavily-populated city:	Sydney, Australia, 3,986,000 inhabitants
Length of coastline:	19,600 km.
Most extensive peninsular:	York, 105,000 sq. km.
Highest mountain:	Mount Wilhelm, Papua New Guinea, 4509 metres
Largest rock in the world:	Ayers Rock, Australia. 348 metres high, 2.5 km. long, 1.6 km. in diameter
Largest island:	New Guinea, 785,000 sq. km.
Largest sandy-based island in the world:	Fraser Island, Australia, 120 km. long
Largest gulf:	Gulf of Carpentaria, 310,000 sq.km.
Largest coral reef in the world:	The Great Barrier Reef, 2027 km.
Lowest place:	Lake Eyre, Australia, 12 metres below sea level
Largest lake:	Lake Eyre, Australia, 9583 sq. km.
Deepest lake:	Manapouri, New Zealand, 443 metres
Longest river:	Murray-Darling, 3490 km.
Largest active volcano:	Mauna Loa, Hawaii, 4,169 sq. km. 9144 metres below sea level
Largest waterfall:	Sutherland, New Zealand, 579 metres
Highest density population:	Nauru, 519 inhabitants per sq. km.
Lowest density population:	Australia, 2.5 inhabitants per sq. km.
Country with the youngest population:	Marshall Islands. 49% of people are less than 15 years old
Country with the oldest population:	Australia, 32% of inhabitants are more than 60 years old
Country with the most men:	Belau, W. Pacific - 115 males for each 100 females
Country with the most women:	New Zealand - 97 males for each 100 females

▶ Records - the continents

Antarctica

Surface area	14,107,637 sq. km.
Population	Consists of people working at scientific stations; 1000 to 5000 inhabitants, according to the time of the year
Scientific stations	38 - Argentina, 6; Australia, 3; Brazil, 1; Chile, 3; China, 2; France, 1; Germany, 1; Japan, 2; India, 1; Italy, 1; New Zealand, 1; Poland, 1; UK, 6; Russia, 5; USA, 3; South Africa, 1
Highest mountain	Mount Vinson, 5140 metres
Largest active volcano	Erebus, 3784 metres
Most extensive glacier in the world	Lambert Glacier, 64 km. wide and 402 km. long
Lowest temperature ever recorded	Minus 89.6°C Vostok base
Maximum wind speed	300 km. per hour

A lack of water affects many areas of the world

Around the world

Country with the most lakes	Finland - 60,000.
Country with the most motorways	Belgium - 452 km. of motorway for every 100 sq. km.
Largest man-made port in the world	Rotterdam, Holland
Europe's largest producer of coal and potatoes	Poland
Country with the most indented coastline in the world	Norway. Some of its fjords stretch 200km into the mainland.
Country in Europe with the most peaks higher than 4,000 metres	Switzerland, 33
Highest waterfall in Europe.	Staubbach Falls, Lauterbrunnen, Switzerland. 350 metres
Country with highest percentage of agricultural workers in Europe	Albania
Most industralized country in Asia.	Japan
Largest National Park in Africa.	The Tsavo National Park, Kenya
Country with the three largest lakes in Africa	Tanzania - Lakes Victoria, Tanganyika and Nyasa.
Highest active geyser in the world	Yellowstone Park, Wyoming, water spurting up to a height of 115 metres.
World's largest freshwater lake.	Lake Superior, between Canada and USA
World's largest producer of tin	Bolivia
Smallest island state in the world	Nauru, Oceania
Largest saltwater lake in the world	The Caspian Sea, Kazakhstan - 371,000 sq. km.

RECORD NEWS
THE
EARTH

Assault on the mythical mountain

The conquest of Everest by New Zealand mountaineer *Edmund Hillary* and Nepalese Sherpa *Tensing Norgay* over half a century ago is still seen as one of the most important achievements of all time.

There had been many attempts at reaching the summit of Everest before. Following unsuccessful expeditions in 1921 and 1922, two British mountaineers, Mallory and Irvine launched a further assault on the mountain in 1924. From markers which were later discovered, it is known that they climbed just beyond 8534 metres of the total height of 8848 metres. They failed to return, and the body of Mallory was only recovered a few years ago.

Colonel Sir John Hunt led the expedition in which Edmund Hillary and Tensing Norgay successfully reached the summit. This prompted many other expeditions to be planned, including a team of US mountaineers in 1963, a British team in 1975, and a Japanese team in 1980.

The record for the number of expeditions reached its peak in 2001, when 182 mountaineers reached the summit of 'the roof of the world' - many more than the 142 climbs of 2000 and the 116 successful expeditions in 1999.

We do not know if the number of climbs will continue each year. What we do know is that mountaineers will always continue to climb Everest, no matter how many further expeditions are planned and how many times Everest is climbed. This great mountain represents the greatest challenge to human endurance and mountaineering skill.

WORLD RECORDS
SPACE

Beyond the Earth

Left: three stages of the formation of a star.
Below: what the Big Bang probably looked like.

There are more stars in the Universe than there are grains of sands on all the beaches in the world. The Universe is so vast that a ray of light travelling from a remote part of Outer Space takes millions of years to reach the Earth. So, when astronomers observe the most distant galaxies, they see them as they were when they were formed, millions and millions of years ago – only one billion years after the birth of the Universe itself. Radio-telescopes are used to study these galaxies, and the further away they are, the further back we look in time.

The constellation of Pleiades (the 'Seven Sisters')

The origin of the Universe

15 billion years ago and within the tiniest length of time – something like a millionth of a billionth of a billionth of a second, there was an explosion in Space. This explosion is known as the **Big Bang**. This was when the Universe began, instantly expanding at a temperature of billions of billions of billions of degrees and rapidly becoming billions and billions and billions times more vast.

Most scientists believe in the theory of the Big Bang, but there are some who talk of *'cosmic strings'* (long strands of are mass energy), of *'parallel dimensions'*, and of a never-ending *expansion-contraction*. In the future, we may know more...

ENORMOUS MEASUREMENTS

Our **Sun** is only one star among an estimated 200 billion stars which orbit in a galaxy called the **Milky Way**. The Earth is also part of this galaxy. The Milky Way is like an enormous belt in Space with branches and spirals 60,000 light years away. (One light year equals about 9.5 million, million kilometres – the distance which light travels in one year.) The Milky Way is only one of about 50 billion galaxies in the Universe and these galaxies are part of huge masses of galaxies. The largest known mass of galaxies in the Universe extends 650 million light years into Outer Space.

FACT

Space is so vast that the most powerful space rocket would take at least 100,000 years to reach the star nearest the Sun!

Far away and 'near'

Venus is the nearest planet to Earth. **Andromeda** is the nearest galaxy. Both are visible to the naked eye (without a telescope or binoculars). At least another 3000 heavenly bodies can be seen from the Earth on a clear night, from a distance of 40 million kilometres to 2.8 million light years. The **Moon** is the nearest heavenly body to our planet, and **Proxima Centauri,** part of the constellation **Centaurus,** is the nearest star – 'only' 4.3 light years away.

FACT

There are many hundreds of groups of stars outside the **Milky Way.** Of these, the group of stars called the **Pleiades** (sometimes called the 'Seven Sisters') is the nearest to Earth, 400 light years from our planet.

Above: the centre of the Milky Way, surrounded by a ring of cosmic gas.

Below: our galaxy, the Milky Way.

THE CONSTELLATIONS

A constellation is a group of stars with a particular shape or pattern. There are 88 **constellations** *in the part of the sky which we can see from Earth. The largest of these constellations is* **Hydra,** *which covers a surface equal to 3.16% of the whole sky and has at least 68 stars. The smallest of these is the* **Southern Cross** *which takes up a 'space' equal to 0.16% of the entire sky.*

Giant stars, shooting stars

The famous Halley's Comet

Stars can be medium-sized, such as our **Sun,** but there are also 'giants' and 'dwarfs'. To get some idea of size – if our Sun were as large as a football, a 'giant' star would be as big as a ball large enough to contain a small city, and a 'dwarf' star would be the size of a billiard ball. **Betelgeuse** is a 'super-giant' star with a diameter 750 times larger than that of our Sun.

Betelgeuse is part of the constellation **Orion.** **Antares** in the **Scorpius** constellation is another 'super-giant', 640 times larger than the Sun.
Even more distant are stars with old, mythical names – **Mira, (Cetus constellation), Deneb, (Cygnus), Aldebaran (Taurus)** and **Canopus,** (also known as Alpha Carinas) a star

FACT

The largest **comet** ever seen passed near the Sun in 1843. Its tail was over 330 million kilometres long and it went from the Sun on to Mars.

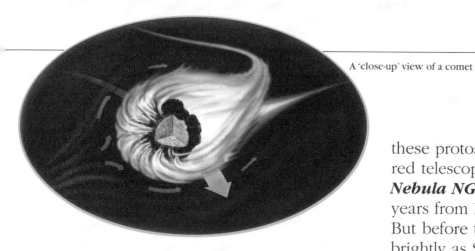
A 'close-up' view of a comet

these protostars can only be detected by infra-red telescopes. These protostars are in the **Nebula NGC 1333**, at a distance of 1100 light years from Earth.

But before these protostars can sparkle as brightly as Sirius, at least another 100,000 years must pass.

The oldest stars in the Milky Way – about seventy of them – are at the top of the disc of the galaxy, formed about a billion years after the **Big Bang**, around 14 billion years ago.

in the **Carina Constellation** and second only to **Sirius** (the 'dog star') for brightness. The 'youngest' stars in the **Milky Way** are two protostars called **IRAS-4. IRAS** stands for **Infra-Red Astronomy Satellite**, because

Stars with a tail

Comets are found at the very edges of the Solar System, where it is colder than we could ever imagine. A comet has the appearance of a great big 'dirty snowball'. The larger comets take thousands of years to complete their orbit around the Sun – for instance, **Encke's Comet** takes 3302 years and **Pons-Winnecke's Comet**, 6125 years. Other comets return close to the Sun at intervals of centuries or decades.

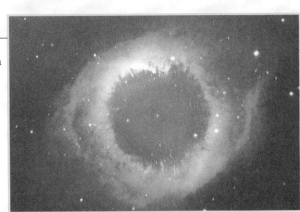
The Helix nebula

Faster than light

In the Universe, a beam of light travels faster than anything else. The **Sun,** the **Earth** and the whole **Solar System** orbit around at the centre of the Milky Way, at an incredible speed of 900,000 kilometres per hour. Yet, in just one second, light travels at least 300,000 kilometres. In one hour, it can cover a distance equal to 1078 million kilometres. In one year, light travels about 9.5 million, million kilometres – a distance which astronomers usually define as one **light year.** So, the time taken for light to travel from **Earth** to the **Moon** is about 1.3 seconds, to reach Pluto, six hours, and, to go on to the edges of our galaxy, the **Milky Way,** 100,000 years. For light from the Earth to land within **Andromeda,** our nearest galaxy, would take 2.8 million years. To reach the limits of the Universe light would take 15 billion years, to the time when we believe the Universe began.

The brightest heavenly bodies

The brightest star in the sky is **Sirius** which the ancient Greeks knew as 'the shining one'. Sirius is part of the constellation **Canis Major** and is about twice as large and 20 times brighter than our Sun. But the heavenly body which is the brightest in the whole of Space is **quasar HS 1946+7658** – which is 15 times brighter than the Sun. (A quasar is the nucleus of a very old galaxy which sends out radio waves and travels at a speed close to the speed of light.) At the other end of the scale, the darkest heavenly bodies, the **obscure nebulae,** can just about be seen.

FACT

An expert driver at the wheel of a racing car travelling at top speed would need an endless supply of fuel and would take 340 billion years – 25 times more than the age of the Universe – to reach the 'finishing line' at the centre of the Milky Way.

WHERE TEETH WOULD CHATTER...

A nebula is a cloud of dust and gas in space. The **Boomerang nebula,** *so-called because the nebula is boomerang-shaped, is 5000 light years distant from the Earth and one of the coldest places in the Universe, where a temperature of -426°C has been recorded. But even this is mild, compared to the temperature of* **Triton,** *one of the moons of Neptune, with an average temperature of -495°C by day.*

Observing the universe

The Hubble Deep Field shows the most distant images in space

To observe Space, astronomers use highly sophisticated optical instruments, such as *telescopes.* Simple binoculars today have approximately the same power to observe the night sky as *Galileo's telescope,* invented in 1610. The most highly-developed telescope in use today is the **Hubble Space Telescope** which orbits at the highest level of the atmosphere and transmits to Earth the clearest images of heavenly bodies ever seen. The Hubble Space Telescope is about the same size as a bus and it completes an entire orbit around the Earth every 90 minutes. *Chandra,* the most powerful X-ray telescope in the world, has an orbit which is 200 times more far-reaching than the Hubble Space Telescope. Imagine a car-driver being able to identify and read an ordinary street map at a distance of 20 kilometres and you get some idea of Chandra's power in receiving images in Space.

Left, Galileo's telescope.

Below, the *Hubble Space Telescope*

The Arecibo radio-telescope

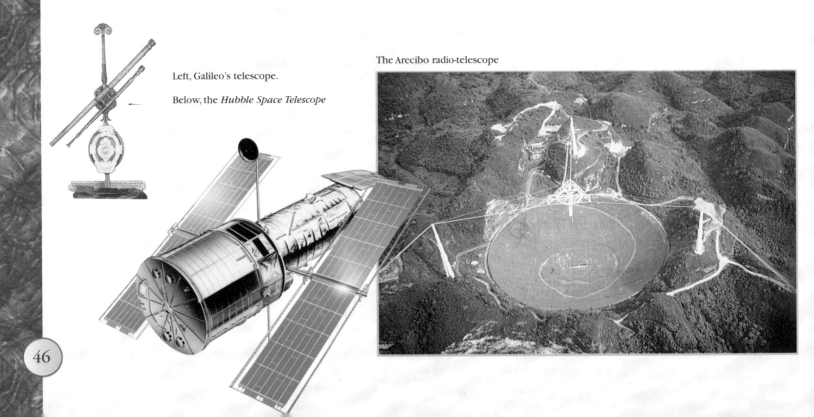

ever seen with a telescope – including heavenly bodies in formation.

The two **Keck telescopes** at the **Mauna Kea Observatory** in Hawaii are the largest optical telescopes in the world, with mirrors 10 metres in diameter within their enormous, huge domes.

The **Very Large Array** in New Mexico (US) is the most modern and one of the largest radio-telescopes in use. Its 27 enormous antennae capture each radio signal transmitted from planets, stars, galaxies and space vehicles. In 1974, astronomers sent signals from the radio-telescope **Arecibo** to **M13,** a star cluster so distant that, should space aliens eventually receive the message, their answer would not reach Earth until about the year 44,000. After the year 2007, the **Next Generation Space Telescope** will be launched into lunar orbit. This will use a mirror 8 metres in diameter which will have different sections. Each section will be able to open and turn out towards Space like the petals of a flower. Then we shall see more beautiful things!

The six telescopes of the *Darwin Space Project.* In the near future these will enable important discoveries to be made outside the Solar System.

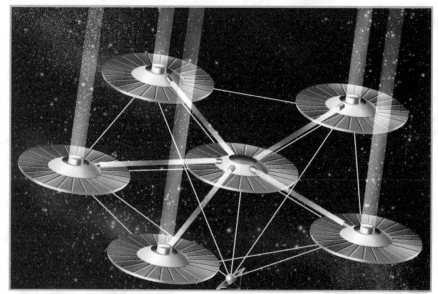

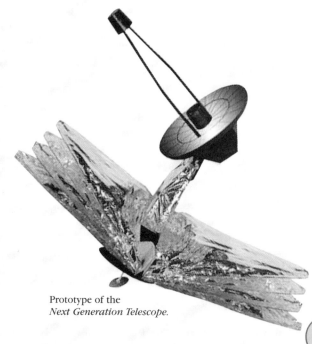

Prototype of the
Next Generation Telescope.

The solar system

The **Solar System** (illustrated on the right), is made up of the **Sun** and a large number of heavenly bodies which orbit (travel around) it. These heavenly bodies include 9 **planets,** 61 **moons, asteroids, comets** and a huge quantity of **dust** and **gas,** which is all that remains of **cosmic clouds** that originated about 5 billion years ago.

THE SUN

The **Sun** *is a star, like billions of other stars in the galaxy. Although it is only a small star, it constitutes about 99.99% of the entire Solar System and could contain the Earth about 1,400,000 times! The Sun is composed mainly of hydrogen and helium. The nuclear pressure within the Sun is up to 2000 billion times more than that registered on the Earth's surface. Its temperature hovers around 14 million degrees Centigrade. The external layer of the Sun, the* **photosphere,** *has a thickness of around 300 kilometres and reaches a heat of 5000°C.*

From the first appearance of the dinosaurs, over 200 million years ago, the Sun has completed just one entire orbit around the Milky Way...

The different phases of formation of the planets.

FACT

In one second, the **Sun** generates more energy than that which has been consumed by the human race in the course of its entire history. A powerful cross-country vehicle, launched into Space at top speed would take 170 years to go from the Earth to the Sun.

Asteroids

Orbiting around the **Sun** and between the planets **Mars** and **Jupiter,** there are thousands of rocky masses (about 4000 of which we know about). These rocky masses are called **asteroids** – some so distant from each other, that if we could travel on a spacecraft into the region of space where asteroids are most numerous, we might not even see one. **Ceres,** the largest asteroid, has a diameter of 1000 kilometres. But there are others with diameters of 100 kilometres. The smallest asteroid known so far, **1993 KA2,** has a diameter of barely 5 metres. If all the asteroids in the Solar System were put together, their combined size would be less than a third of the Moon.

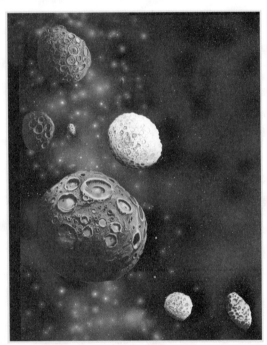

Asteroids never travel alone through space. Instead, they group together in great masses, something like that depicted in the illustration on the left. Below, a rocky object from the 'asteroid belt' in Space. To the right, a meteorite as it crashes into another object in space.

FACT

The largest **meteorite** (fragment of an asteroid falling to Earth) was found in Africa, in Namibia. It was 2.7 metres long by 2.4 metres wide and weighed over 60 tonnes... as heavy as 11 elephants!

GIANT STONES, FALLING STARS

A whole multitude of small rocks, fragments of comets, orbit around the **Sun.** *These rocky fragments are called meteors. Each day some collide with other heavenly bodies, or fall to Earth, when they are defined as* **meteorites.** *It is estimated that only about once in tens of millions of years would a meteorite be large enough to cause a disaster. More often, a meteorite is only as big as a stone. The largest crater made by a meteorite is the* **Meteor Crater** *in Arizona, USA. This crater measures more than 1200 metres in diameter, 183 metres deep, and is believed to have been made about 50,000 years ago.*

Mercury

Mercury is the planet nearest the Sun. By day, within the craters on its surface, the temperature averages between 350-400°C. But by night, this drops to at least -170°C due to the lack of atmosphere. Mercury's nucleus of iron and nickel is larger than the Moon. The **Caloris Basin,** one of Mercury's craters, is half as large as the whole of North America.

Mercury orbits around the Sun on a very stretched-out, elongated orbit at a much faster speed than any other planet. It has a diameter of 4878 kilometres and one day on Mercury lasts the equivalent to 58.6 days on Earth – which means that Mercury has a year equal to 88 Earth days. The average distance from Mercury to the Sun is 58 million kilometres.

Venus

After the Sun and the Moon, the planet **Venus** is the brightest heavenly body seen from the Earth. It is also the hottest and most inhospitable planet in the entire Solar System. Surrounded by a thick blanket of cloud, and with a dense atmosphere of carbon dioxide, its vast plain has 167 extremely high volcanoes on the surface, some over 8000 metres high. The ground temperature of Venus is at least 480°C – hot enough to melt even lead. It is constantly battered by sulphuric acid rain and the pressure of the air is at least 90 times that of the Earth. The diameter of Venus is 12,104 kilometres, and one Venus day equals 243 days on Earth. One year on Venus lasts as long as 225 Earth years. The average distance from Venus to the Sun is 108 million kilometres.

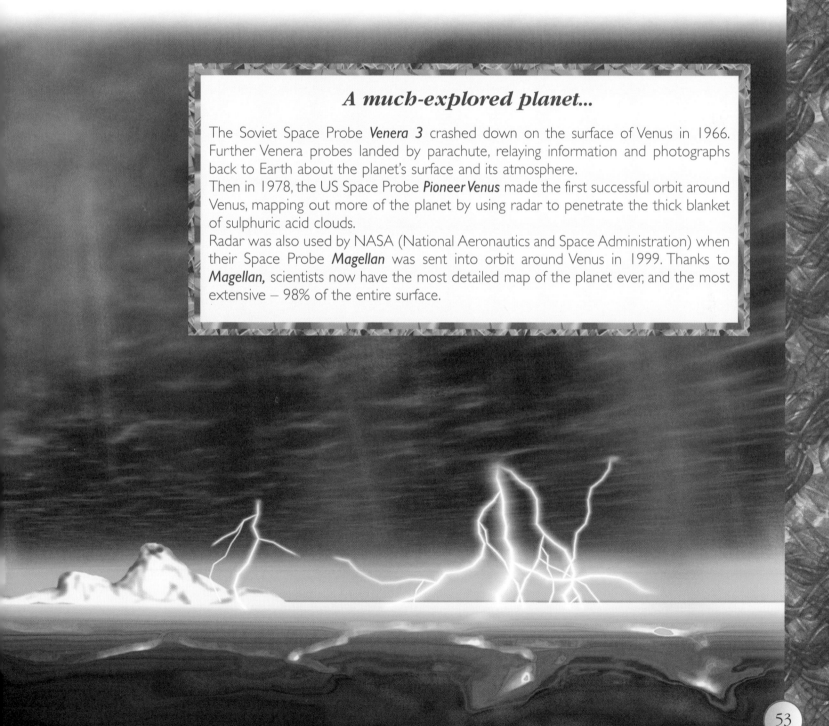

A much-explored planet...

The Soviet Space Probe **Venera 3** crashed down on the surface of Venus in 1966. Further Venera probes landed by parachute, relaying information and photographs back to Earth about the planet's surface and its atmosphere.

Then in 1978, the US Space Probe **Pioneer Venus** made the first successful orbit around Venus, mapping out more of the planet by using radar to penetrate the thick blanket of sulphuric acid clouds.

Radar was also used by NASA (National Aeronautics and Space Administration) when their Space Probe **Magellan** was sent into orbit around Venus in 1999. Thanks to **Magellan,** scientists now have the most detailed map of the planet ever, and the most extensive – 98% of the entire surface.

Earth

The diameter of the **Earth** is 12,756 kilometres. One day lasts 24 hours, there are 365.26 days in each year, and the average distance from the Sun is 149.6 kilometres. Earth has an internal nucleus of solid iron, very, very hot and with a thickness of 1000 kilometres. Its external nucleus is liquid iron, 2400 kilometres thick.

The external nucleus is surrounded by a rocky 'mantle' 2800 kilometres down into the depths of the planet and then a surface crust, rather like the skin of a fruit. Earth's crust is 35 kilometres thick beneath the continents and 5-10 kilometres thick beneath the oceans.

FACT

In its orbit around the Sun, Earth travels at a speed of 30 kilometres per second – 1800 kilometres per minute – at the same time spinning on its own axis at 1700 kilometres per hour. The drilling at a platinum mine at **Zapolyarny** in Russia holds the record for excavation, digging down to a depth of 15 kilometres – just a 'scratch' on the crust of the Earth. Digging at a rate of 10 centimetres each minute, it would take a good 261 years to dig a tunnel through the Earth – if such a feat were possible!

THE MOON

The diameter of the **Moon** is about one quarter that of the Earth (3476 kilometres). The average distance from Earth is 384,000 kilometres. The surface of the Moon covers the same area as the continent of Africa, with a temperature which varies between -155°C and -105°C. The force of gravity is equal to one sixth of that on Earth – so, on the Moon, a person weighs six times less than on Earth, which means a human being can jump higher than a kangaroo, making footprints which last millions of years... On the surface of the Moon, it does not rain and the wind does not blow! Moon is Earth's satellite, and so far, it is the only heavenly body on which humans have landed.

Mars

Mars is the fourth planet from the Sun at a distance of 228 million kilometres. It leans at an angle in its orbit, in a similar way to Earth. Mars also has ice-caps and seasons similar to that of our 'blue planet' and a temperature at its Equator which in summer can reach 20°C. More often the climate remains stable below zero, falling to -80°C by night.

Olympus Mons is an ancient volcano on Mars, now extinct. It is the highest mountain in the whole Solar System, three times higher than Mount Everest. The **Valles Marineris** is a canyon which is so long that the Grand Canyon in Arizona seems like a small scratch. One day on the 'red planet' lasts 24.6 Earth hours, one year 687 Earth days, and its diameter is 6794 kilometres.

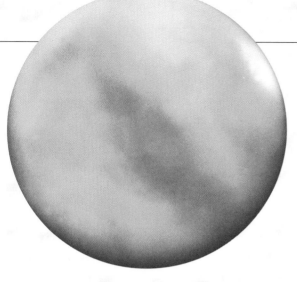

THE MOONS OF MARS

*Around **Mars** orbit two small moons shaped rather like giant potatoes – **Phobos** at 28 kilometres diameter and **Deimos** with a diameter of 16 kilometres, the smallest satellite in the Solar System and 40 million times smaller than our Moon. The force of gravity on Deimos is so weak that if any future space travellers were to jump on its surface, they would find themselves flying off into Space.*

FACT

If the ice on **Mars** were to melt, its surface would be flooded by an ocean with depths of between 10 and 100 metres.

Europa

Jupiter

Jupiter is the largest planet in the Solar System – so large that our Earth could fit inside it more than 1000 times! The planet is covered by a thick layer of cloud and strong winds whirl around a sphere made up of a small rocky nucleus and a thick mantle of gas. Jupiter's diameter is 142,800 kilometres, one day lasts 9.8 Earth hours, and one year equals 11.8 Earth years. The average distance from the Sun is 778 million kilometres.

FACT

The **Great Red Spot** is an enormous cyclone which shakes the whole planet at least once every 300 years. Compared to its power and strength, the most devastating hurricane on Earth would only be a puff of wind....

The Moons of Jupiter

Jupiter boasts at least 16 moons. The largest four, *Ganymede, Callisto, Io* and *Europa* were discovered in 1610 by Galileo Galilei. *Ganymede* is the largest satellite in the entire Solar System, 2017 larger than our Moon, and even as large as planets such as Mercury and Pluto. *Io* is entirely covered by volcanoes which shoot out jets of liquid sulphur with more force than a missile shot from a fire-arm.

Saturn

From Earth, **Saturn** appears to be circled by thousands of rings. These rings are made up of hundreds of thousands of blocks of ice and rocks, the largest as big as a six-storey house. Saturn is made up mainly of helium and hydrogen at gaseous, liquid and solid state, and winds blow at a force of 1800 kilometres an hour.

Less dense than all the other planets, Saturn seems to be sunken in a great big ocean, making the planet appear yellow within it. The diameter of Saturn is 119,300 kilometres, the diameter of its rings at least 273,700 kilometres. On Saturn, one day lasts 10.2 Earth hours and one year equals 29.5 Earth years. The average distance from the Sun is estimated at 1427 million kilometres.

FACT

Of the 15 moons of **Uranus,** 10 were discovered only in 1986, thanks to the American Space Probe **Voyager 2.** The largest satellite, **Oberon**, has an impressive diameter of 1630 kilometres. And on the surface of the second largest moon, **Miranda,** there are craters ten times deeper than the Grand Canyon. The other moons each have a diameter of less than 80 kilometres.

Uranus

The axis of Uranus tilts back at 60°. This means that, within the space of one year on the planet, and which corresponds to 84 Earth years, both poles are illuminated constantly for 42 years, with a dark and constant night lasting the next 42 years. Uranus is four times larger than Earth, with 11 rings, just a few thousand metres thick and made up of millions of particle masses encircling its equator. The diameter of Uranus is 51,800 kilometres and one day lasts 17.2 hours on Earth. The average distance from Uranus to the Sun is 2870 million kilometres.

Right: Voyager 2 whilst in transit towards Uranus, 24 January 1986. Below, the surface of the planet.

The moons of Saturn

Saturn has the most moons – an astonishing 18! *Titan* is the second largest satellite in the Solar System, just a little smaller than *Ganymede*, one of the moons of Jupiter. One third of the surface of its satellite *Mimas* is covered by giant craters.

Neptune

Blanketed by thin clouds and encircled by a slender band of rings, **Neptune** boasts 8 moons. Its diameter is 49,500 kilometres, one day lasts 16.1 Earth hours, and one year on Neptune lasts 164.8 Earth years – far longer than the life of a human being. The average distance from Neptune to the Sun is 4497 kilometres.

Image of a Space Probe of a mission to explore the planets Neptune and Pluto within the next few years.

FACT

Pluto has just one giant moon – **Charon**, with a diameter of at least 1200 kilometres and its surface made up of ice as hard as rock.

Pluto

Pluto is the smallest planet and very cold (-280°C average temperature). It is the most distant in the Solar System. Its orbit is quite different to that of any of the other planets, slanting so much that, over a period of twenty years, this planet is sometimes to be found within the orbit of Neptune, as if on a 'heavenly roundabout'. Pluto's moon, **Charon,** is half as large as the planet itself, and it is the most distant satellite in the entire Solar System. The diameter of Pluto is 2300 kilometres and one day on the planet is equal to 6.4 days on Earth, with one year equal to 248 Earth years. The average distance from the Sun is 5915 kilometres. From the surface of Pluto, the Sun appears as a far distant and extremely bright star.

The Moons of Neptune

The largest of **Neptune's** 8 moons is **Triton** (shown in the illustration). Triton is the coldest place in all the Solar System -495°C. Despite the ice-covered surface, Triton shoots powerful jets of liquid oxygen into the face of the Universe, rather like a natural geyser on Earth. It is the only satellite which orbits its planet in the opposite direction to the movement of its rotation.

The conquest of space

4 October 1957	The Soviet Union launched the first artificial satellite, **Sputnik 1**. For the first time on 3 November of the same year, the Soviet Union sent a living thing – **a dog called Laika** – into space on board **Sputnik 2**.
31 January 1958	The USA launched their first artificial satellite, **Explorer 1**.
2 January 1958	Russian-built **Lunik 1** became the first artificial satellite to leave Earth's orbit and to pass over the Moon. On 12 September, **Lunik 2** became the first Space Probe to make a landing on the surface of the Moon. On 7 October of the same year, **Lunik 3** sent back the first photographic images of the 'hidden side' of the Moon.
1 April 1960	The USA launched the first weather satellite, **Tiros 1**.
12 April 1961	**Yuri A. Gagarin** on board the spacecraft **Vostok 1**, was the first man in space, orbiting around the Earth for 1 hour and 48 minutes.
20 February 1962	**John Glenn**, on board spacecraft **Mercury 6**, became the first American in orbit around the Earth. His space mission lasted about 5 hours.
6 July 1962	The USA launched the first telecommunications satellite, **Telstar 1**.

Sputnik 1   Spacecraft *Mercury*   *Apollo 11*. The Conquest of the Moon

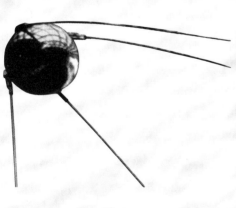
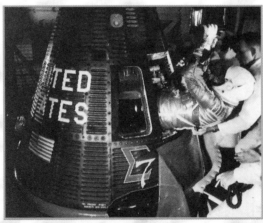

Space-Station *MIR*

3 October 1962   American astronaut **W. M. Schirra Jr.**, on board the spacecraft **Mercury 8**, established a record which is so far unbeaten. After completing 6 orbits around the Earth within a time of just over 8 hours, he then made a successful landing at 'just' 7 kilometres from the expected location.

16 June 1963   Russian **Valentina V. Tereskova**, on board **Vostok 6**, became the first woman in Space.

12 October 1964   Spacecraft **Voskhod 1** (USSR) was the first space vehicle with three cosmonauts on board.

18 March 1965   Soviet cosmonaut **A. Leonov**, on board the space mission **Voskhod 2**, completed the first 'walk' in space, leaving his spacecraft for ten minutes.

15 December 1965   USA spacecrafts *Gemini* 6 and *Gemini* 7 completed the first 'meeting' in orbit in the history of space flight.

24 December 1968   **Apollo 8**, with American astronauts **F. Borman**, **J. Lovell** and **W. Anders** on board, completed the first orbital flight around the Moon.

Voyager   *Space Shuttle*   *Galileo* Space Probe   *Hubble* Space Telescope

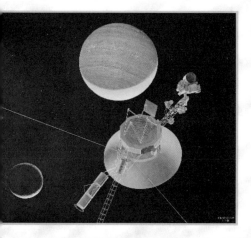

▶ The conquest of space

21 July 1969   As part of the USA *Apollo Space Programme*, American Astronauts **N. Armstrong** and **E. Aldrin**, members of the team aboard **Apollo 11**, made the first landing on the Moon. During their time on Lunar soil (21 hours, 36 minutes and 21 seconds), they collected 22 kilograms of rock samples and other materials.
Following this, another 5 Apollo missions were to take men to the Moon. Thanks to the lunar modules, a further 10 astronauts were able to set foot on the Moon, collecting over 400 kg of rock samples and completing over 280 excursions each lasting many hours and over a dozen days.

14 May 1973   **Skylab 1**, the first American Space Station was launched into orbit.

17 July 1975   As part of the joint American and Soviet space programme *Apollo-Soyuz*, spacecraft **Apollo 18** reached and coupled up with **Soyuz**, which was already in orbit. The spacecrafts were able to exchange crew members and experiment with working together.

An astronaut at work outside the space cabin.

12 April 1981	The USA launched into orbit the first reusable spacecraft or 'Space Shuttle', **Space Shuttle *Columbia***, with astronauts **R. Crippen** and **J. Young** on board. After a flight of 36 hours, ***Columbia*** landed safely in the Californian Desert.
April 1983	On the occasion of the first test of the Space Shuttle ***Challenger***, US astronauts **S. Musgrave** and **D. Paterson** completed the first walk in space.
21 December 1988	The two Soviet cosmonauts **B. Titov** and **M. Manarov**, established a permanent record in Space on board the Space Station **MIR** in orbit from February 1986; 365 days, 22 hours and 40 minutes.
April 1990	The Space Shuttle ***Discovery*** carried in orbit the first Space Telescope, the **Hubble Space Telescope**.
31 July 1992	Space Shuttle ***Atlantis*** was launched on Mission STS-46. On board – **Claude Nicollier**, first Swiss astronaut in space, **Franco Malerba**, first Italian astronaut, **Franklin R. Chang-Diaz**, first Costa-Rican, female astronaut **Marsha S. Ivins**, (US) and US crew member **Jeffrey A. Hoffman**, with Commander **Loren J. Shriver** (US) and Pilot **Andrew M. Allen** (US).
8 July 1994	The crew on board ***Columbia*** established the record of permanent orbit in a Space Shuttle – 353 hours and 55 minutes. In February of the same year there began the first combined Russian-American Space Programme for the construction of a Space Station.
6 February 1995	The first meeting in Space between the Russian Space Station **MIR** (meaning 'peace') and the American Space Shuttle ***Discovery***. On 22 March, Russian cosmonaut **V. Poliakov** returned to Earth on board ***Soyuz 21***, after having spent over 439 days on a Space Station – an astonishing record!
29 June 1995	The Space Shuttle ***Atlantis*** linked up with **MIR** in the first of seven space meetings, exchanging crews and beginning a plan of work and joint experiments.
29 October 1998	**John Glenn**, the first American to be launched into orbit on 20 February 1962, established a new record on board the Space Shuttle ***Discovery***. At 77 years old, he became the oldest astronaut ever to have taken part in a Space Mission.
23 July 1999	The July 1999 mission by the Space Shuttle ***Columbia*** was the first in the history of Space exploration to have a woman commander – **Eileen M. Collins**.
1 February 2003	American Space Shuttle ***Columbia*** disintegrated in space, approximately 61,400 metres above Texas, USA. All six members of the crew were killed – American astronauts, commander **Rick Husband**, pilot **William McCool**, mission specialists **Michael Anderson**, **David Brown**, **Laurel Clark** and **Kalpana Chawla**, and Israel's first man in space, **Ilan Roman**, payload specialist.

Michael Collins

Neil Armstrong

The I. S. S.

The **International Space Station (or I.S.S.)** is a most important development in space exploration. Led jointly by NASA and the Russian Space Agency, a total of 16 countries are taking part. NASA astronauts and Russian cosmonauts have been working in four-month shifts at I.S.S. for the past few years, and the Station is expected to be fully completed in 2006.

The **I.S.S.** will eventually be as large as a football pitch (108.5 metres long and 88.4 metres wide), four times larger than the Soviet Space Station **MIR**.

The **I.S.S.** is being assembled in space. American and Russian space shuttles transport into space the most sophisticated materials and instruments, with astronauts completing the assembly. In 1998 astronauts Winston E. Scott (US) and Takao Doi (Japan) tested tools and equipment for future Space Station assembly during the course of two space walks.

The **I.S.S.** will orbit at a height of 400 - 500 kilometres from the Earth and remain in orbit for about 10 years. On board will be six research laboratories manned by an international team of 7 - 8 scientists.

20 July 1969, Neil Armstrong descends from the lunar module and completes the first walk on the Moon.

MOON GOLF...

*From 1969 to 1972, 12 astronauts from the American Space Mission **Apollo** have landed on the Moon. One member of the 1971 **Apollo 14** Mission was Alan Shepard, who, on 5 May 1961, on board **Freedom** 7, became the first American to go into space at a height of 185 kilometres above the Earth. Ten years later, on the Moon, Alan Shepard used an instrument for gathering up moon samples as a golf club. He hit a stone out towards one of the many enormous gaps in space - and, as he did so, the surrounding surface of the Moon suddenly shone with a greenish hue.*

FACT

During the assembly of the Italian cargo carrier space shuttle *Leonardo* for the I.S.S. US astronauts Jim Voss and Susan Helms established a new record for a spacewalk – 8 hours and 56 minutes – on 11 March 2001.

Interplanetary journeys

Starting from 1957, there have been over 200 space missions. Apart from the space programmes with the objective of landing on the Moon, most of these missions have usually incorporated Space Probes, artificial satellites, modules, robots or special space vehicles with fascinating names (**Mariner**, **Venera**, **Vega**, **Pioneer**) all destined to reach and to explore the planets of the Solar System. Most heavenly bodies - such as comets and asteroids - are too far distant to be reached by human beings. For example, the **Apollo** spacecraft which took about three Earth days to reach the Moon, would take 850,000 Earth years to come within sight of the nearest star. It was in the 1970s that Space Probes first reached the planets Venus and Mars, and exploration of other planets soon followed.

Some Space Probes are only able to orbit around the planet in order to make observations and take photographs, such as the Space Probe **Magellan** did, on its orbit around Venus. Others, such as the capsule unhooked from Space Probe **Galileo** on Jupiter, can examine the atmosphere of a planet, before landing on the surface. Some Space Probes can land and send back information on the chances of life on a planet or on the physical and chemical nature of its surface - such as the **Mars Pathfinder**, with its robot-controlled six-wheeled vehicle **Sojourner** exploring the surface of the 'red planet', carrying out studies of the soil, dust and the rocks and tracing ancient sources of water. There are also Space Probes which make journeys close to planets, before proceeding on their interplanetary journey - for instance, **Voyager 1** and **Voyager 2** (shown left). Both have provided valuable information as well as some remarkable photographs of Jupiter, Saturn, Uranus and Neptune. (Only the planet Pluto has so far never been visited by any artificial satellite.) Voyager 1 and Voyager 2 are now travelling beyond the Solar System, 12 billion kilometres from the Earth. In the Universe, they are the most far distant man-made objects from our planet.

Until now, no Space Probe has ever returned to Earth. Radio contact was soon lost with 15 or more and many others have become damaged beyond repair. The launch of more than 40 Space Probes failed, with the space missions coming to an end during the first phase of flight or even on the launch pad.

FACT

The record for the most distant space flight from the Earth, 400,171 kilometres, still belongs to the unfortunate *Apollo 13*. Because of a breakage in the oxygen tank, the team destined for the Moon had to return, using the landing module.

Countries in orbit

Most space exploration has been done by the ex-Soviet Union with 112 space missions, followed by the United States with 83 missions. In recent years there have been four Japanese space missions, plus the Russian **Mars 96** space mission and eight space missions from **ESA** - the European Space Agency. Only American astronauts have ever set foot on the **Moon**. There have been 106 space missions to the Moon, including those for observing and taking photographs. This total is shared equally by the ex-USSR and the USA. **Venus** has been reached by 40 Space Probes; **Mars** by 37; **Jupiter** and **Saturn** each by 3; **Uranus** and **Neptune** by 1, the **Sun** by at least 6; **Titan**, Saturn's moon, by 1; **Phobos**, Mars' satellite, by 1. In addition to these, a further ten Space Probes have centred on the study of **comets** and at least three on **asteroids**.

Other Space Probes have only been of an experimental nature. Seven have been built, but have never gone outside Earth's orbit.

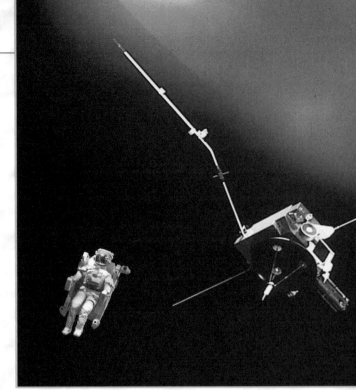

Space Probe *Ulysses* venturing towards the poles of the Sun

Space Probe *Pioneer* journeying towards Venus

Mariner 10 reached Mercury in March 1974

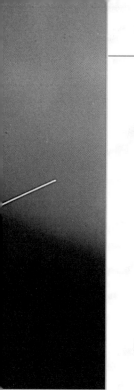

ON THE LAUNCH PAD

In order to leave Earth's surface and enter into orbit, a space vehicle needs an enormous push; booster rockets are fired up into the sky at a speed of 28,000 kilometres an hour! During the launch of a spacecraft, the rocket burns 10 tonnes of fuel per second. The largest rocket ever built is the United States Saturn 5, more than 100 metres tall. It launched the spacecraft Apollo into orbit, weighing 2903 tonnes.

Voyager nears Saturn

Space Probe *Giotto* meets *Halley's Comet* under the eyes of a 'virtual' (computer image) astronaut

A WANDERER IN SPACE

A pressurized spacesuit for extra-vehicular (outside the spacecraft) missions weighs 47 kilograms - the helmet alone weighs at least 4 kilograms. A special liquid is pumped through a network of tubes, 90 metres in length, enabling the astronaut to maintain a constant body temperature, whilst layers of 'kevlar' and 'teflon' protects the astronaut from cosmic radiation and grains of intergalactic dust which travel at over 35,000 kilometres per hour.

The MMU (Manoeuvre Movement Unit) is a sort of flying armchair with 24 push-buttons with which the astronaut can move about in space in much the same way as the EMU (Extra-Vehicular Mobility Unit) a type of small rocket, mounted on the back of the spacesuit, equipped with batteries and a reserve of oxygen, and weighing about 70 kilograms.

Space Probe *Galileo* approaches the asteroid Gospra

Astronauts among the stars

To date, about 400 people have travelled in space. Of these, 254 are American, 93 ex-Soviet Union or Russian, 10 German, 8 Canadian, 8 French, 5 Japanese, 3 Italian, and one each from Cuba, Vietnam, Mongolia, Poland, the former Czechoslovakia; Bulgaria; Hungary, Romania, Holland, Saudi Arabia and Mexico.

Astronauts at work in space. Below, the construction of the *ISS, International Space Station*

Business in space

American businessmen and Russian engineers have joined forces to build the first space shuttle designed exclusively for tourists. The ***Cosmopolis XXI*** Aerospace System or 'C-21' was unveiled to the public at ***Zhukovsky*** Air Base near Moscow. Starting from 2004 - 2005, and for only 99,000 American dollars (a small sum, compared to the 20 million dollars paid by millionaire Dennis Tito to spend one week in the ***I.S.S.*** (International Space Station), a person will be able to have an hour's space flight, experiencing the absence of gravity 100 kilometres above the Earth in a space vehicle about the same size as a mini-bus.

Also, the Moon is arousing business interest, even in countries with large areas of deprivation, such as China and India. With the era of astronauts and dramatic space missions now past, new space enterprises are turning towards examining the structure of the Moon and the lunar subsoil, searching for precious sources of water or deposits of rare minerals, and to the possibility of setting up scientific laboratories. Commercial enterprises, such as the American company ***TransOrbital Inc.*** and ***International Space Company*** have developed their businesses by selling photographic images and the latest maps of space provided by Space Probes.

Satellite business

Telephone communication by satellite began in 1960, when American John Pierce developed ECHO, designed to receive telephone signals and reflect them back to Earth. This was followed by the launch on 10 July 1962 of TELSTAR which enabled television images to be transmitted directly from the USA to TV screens throughout Europe, via the UK and France. We also have to thank artificial satellites for beginning the development of direct transmission by Facsimile (FAX), telephone, telephoto and mobile telephone, as well as weather forecasting and geographical survey.

COMSAT (Communications Satellite Corporation) was founded in the USA in 1962 to develop the business from communications satellites. 17 other countries joined in 1964 to form INTELSAT (International Telecommunication Satellite Consortium) with the aim of establishing a worldwide commercially-based communications network. Membership of INTELSTAT now includes almost all countries in the world. INMARST (International Maritime Satellite Organization) provides communication systems to ships and offshore industries.

RECORD NEWS
SPACE

Space stations

There are over twenty Space Centres in the world. Four are in the US - at *Cape Canaveral-Kennedy*, in Florida: at Houston in Texas, which also houses the Centre for Administration of *NASA;* at *Vanderberg* in California, and at *Wallops Island* in Virginia, used mainly for military purposes. *Cape Canaveral-Kennedy* is the US Space Centre which is mostly used. It was here that the launch of the inaugural US Space Mission took place on 31 January 1958, when the first American artifical satellite, *Explorer,* was launched into orbit.

Another three important Space Centres are located within the former Soviet Union in Russia - *Kapustin-Yar* and *Plesetsk,* and one in Kazakistan, *Bajkonur*. It is the *Bajkonur* Space Centre which holds the record for the highest number of launches (over 40), and it also has been established the longest: here, on 4 October 1957, *Sputnik 1,* the first artificial (man-made) satellite, was launched into space.

Other Space Centres are to be found in Japan - the *Tanegashima Space Center* and the *Kagoshima Space Center*. In India, there is the *ISRO Shriharikotta;* in Israel the *Palmachim;* in Australia, the *Woomera;* in Brazil, *Sao José dos Campos* and *Sao Luis*. In Italy, a small Space Centre, the *San Marco* was established in 1967, and there are also two small platforms anchored off the coast of Kenya in the Indian Ocean.

In 1970, the *ESA* (European Space Agency) established a Launch Centre at Kourou, in French Guyana. This is the most active Launch Centre in the world, and from where the first *Ariane* rocket vehicle was launched. Because of its geographical location north of the Equator, it is possible to launch satellites from this Space Centre to a height of 36,000 kilometres, burning less energy and considerably less fuel. Also, Guyana is an 'anti-seismic' zone, far away from the routes of hurricanes and with a sparse population. Today, the Launch Centre Station at *Kourou* is the central point of all the space missions for the launch of geostationary satellites. Geostationary satellites orbit at the same speed and take the same path as Earth. They are used for telecommunications and for research on launch vehicles and new fuels which will soon enable equipment and instruments weighing 12-13 tonnes to be transported outside Earth's gravity.

Ariane 5, the largest rocket used by *ESA* to launch artificial satellites, was in fact assembled in a hangar and then transferred on to a special launch pad. The whole thing was transported to the launch site, with the least risk of vibration and fire, thanks to a special wagon weighing 1500 tonnes and pulled by a powerful locomotive.

In 1999, the first successful Chinese spacecraft *Shenzhou II* went into orbit around the Earth. Chinese scientists have since forecast that a Chinese astronaut will be in orbit by 2005, with a manned landing on the Moon by 2010. China has three space centres - at *Jiuquan* (from where *Shenzhou II* was launched) and at *Xichang* and *Taiyuan*.

WORLD RECORDS
ANIMALS

Classes of animals...

The mouse is the most common mammal.

The number of species of animal life that we know about is estimated at one and a half million - although it is believed that many more are yet to be discovered. The most numerous are the **invertebrate** (no backbone) **arthropods** (segmented bodies) with almost 900,000 species, of which 800,000 are **insects**. 100,000 arthropods are the species classified as **molluscs**. Among the **vertebrates** (with backbone), the most numerous are **fish**, with 25,000 species, followed by **birds** (8600 species), **reptiles** (6000 species), **mammals** (4500 species) and **amphibians** (3000 species). **Mice** account for more than a quarter of all mammals. The most widespread mammal is our own species, that of **humankind**.

A pair of Muscovy ducks

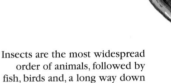

Insects account for over half of the total number of species, mammals only 0.25 %. This means that **insects** constitute one quarter of living things - they are more numerous than all kinds of other species put together.

The order of **coleoptera** (beetles) is the most widespread class of insect - about 90% of the total number.

Insects are the most widespread order of animals, followed by fish, birds and, a long way down the list, mammals.

SPECIES KNOWN SO FAR

As well as the species which are known to us, zoologists and ethnologists estimate that there are between 5 and 30 million species which have not yet been identified. For example - some **Amazon monkeys** *and* **small grass-eaters** *of the tropical rain forest have only recently been classified; and on just one tree in the Amazon rain forest, at least 43 different species of* **ants** *were recently observed. That is the same number of species of ants as there are in the whole of the United Kingdom.*

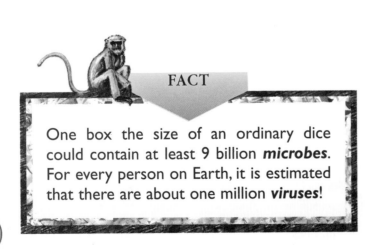

FACT

One box the size of an ordinary dice could contain at least **9 billion microbes**. For every person on Earth, it is estimated that there are about one million **viruses**!

So many different types!

Scientists are constantly trying to calculate the number of different species, or examples of species, of a genus (or family) of animals. The results are amazing. It is calculated that alongside a little less than 5 billion people, there lives on our planet 5000 billion insects - that's at least 5 million million! A combined total of one million worms, earthworms and grubs crawl about in just one hectare of land. There are at least 100 billion fish in our seas, rivers and oceans. Put together, these would weigh an estimated 838 million tonnes. The total number of amphibians is about one billion and the bird population is at least 100 billion. Prehistoric dinosaurs were reptiles. The 2 billion reptiles which survive today are descendents from those creatures who roamed the Earth before human life had even begun to develop.

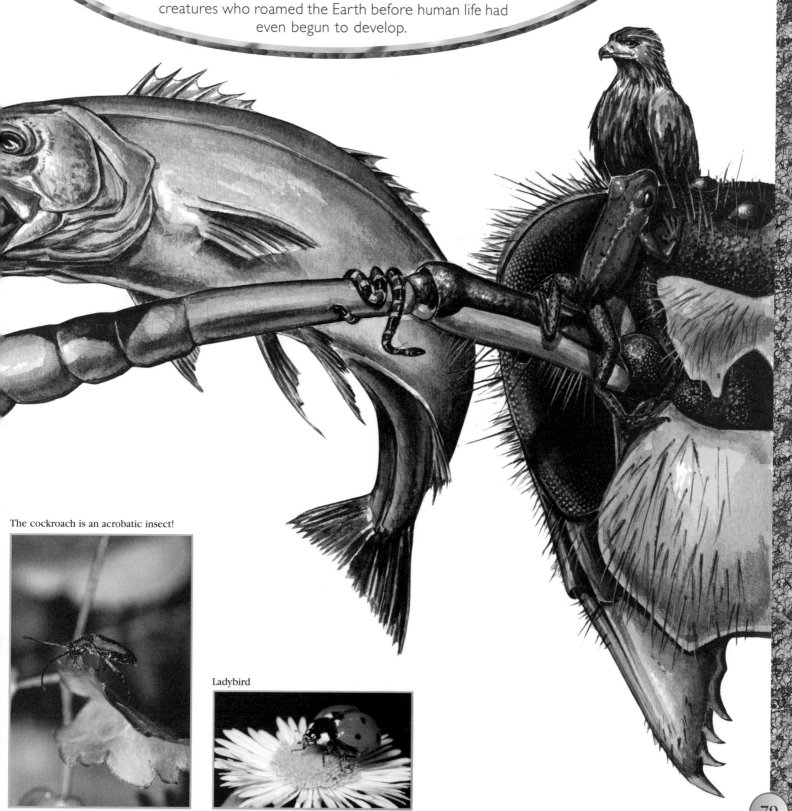

The cockroach is an acrobatic insect!

Ladybird

▶ Classes of animals...

We cannot be sure how many species of animal life have become extinct, nor how many species were made extinct in prehistoric times, before the beginnings of human life. Some scientists believe that more than a thousand species have become extinct within the last 500 years. According to research, animal species at risk of extinction decrease in number at the rate of 27,000 - 40,000 each year, indicating further reductions which will affect almost all classes of vertebrates. Despite widespread extinction among other bird species, there are at least 12 billion **chickens** on Earth - ten times the population of China! The total number of **cows** at any one time is about 1,300,000,000.

The combined number of **sheep** and **goats** is about 2 billion - the majority of which are in Third World countries and in New Zealand - here, there are at least 16 sheep for each inhabitant.

Almost 70% of **ducks**, 400 million, are reared in China, where certain types of these web-footed birds are considered a special treat - like the **turkey** which most Americans enjoy on their Thanksgiving Day. In the USA there are at least 300 million turkeys at any one time.

Duck

Cockerel and Hen

Pigs

FACT

Donkeys were once widely used for farming in eastern countries. Now, in common with **horses** and other **working animals** such as **mules** and **asses**, they have been replaced by more modern farming machines. The donkey population worldwide is now no more than 150 million. **Pigs** are still quite numerous, almost one billion, and the total number of **dromedaries** (one hump) and **camels** (two humps) is estimated at about 20 million, concentrated mainly within one tenth of Asiatic and North African countries.

Turkey

Donkey

Dromedary

PROTOZOA ANIMAL LIFE

Protozoa is often referred to as 'the lowest form of animal life' because each animal in this class is composed of just one cell. There are at least 30,800 species of protozoa, widespread throughout all regions of the Earth. They are the smallest living things of all and they live mostly in water. Among the best-known species of protozoa are - the **amoeba**, **nematode** ('eelworm'), **cyclops**, **rotifero**, **paramecium** and **water fleas** (shown in the picture).

Protozoa such as the **foraminiferan** and **radiolara** can assume strange, incredible shapes. Others can be ugly and harmful, as in the case of the **plasmodium**, a species of **parasitic protozoa** which are carriers of dangerous diseases such as malaria.

In the Sahara Desert... on the back of a donkey!

81

The slowest

The slow pace of the **snail** is well-known! In one day it travels a maximum of ten metres, and then only on a level surface. But even this is impressive, compared to the limpet, a mollusc (an invertebrate with non-segmented body) which lives stuck fast to a rock. From dawn to sunset, the **limpet** moves no more than one thirtieth of a centimetre. The 'laziness' of the **sloth** is founded on fact. It may stay drowsing among the branches of a tree for whole days. But then, this plant-eating mammal can move at the rate of 2.5 metres per minute! That is equal to 3.5 kilometres a day!

But it is the **koala** which is the record-breaking lazybones! This small mammal sleeps at least 22 hours each day.

Sea horses can never claim a lightning speed. Instead they travel calmly among the waters, quite unhurried and at a speed equal to about 1.5 metres per hour.

Koala

Sloth

The flea has no rival in jumping high. The kangaroo rat jumps the furthest and the locust jumps the most upright.

Snail

FACT

The animal with the largest heart is the **Blue Whale**. It is the largest animal on Earth. Its weight can be more than 200 tonnes, including its heart which weighs 100 kg.

Booby

GOLD MEDAL PROSPECTS

*Even smaller or little-known species can be record-holders in the animal world. For example - the undisputed champion of divers is the **Booby**, a sea bird which can dive down from a height of over 40 metres to catch a tiny fish. The **flea** is unbeatable when it comes to jumping high. At just 1.5 millimetres long, it can jump over 20 centimetres, 130 times its own height! The best long-jumper is the **Kangaroo Rat**, a marsupial (animal with a pouch) which can clear 6 - 7 metres in one jump, over 10 times its length, and more than 20 times the length of its tail.*

*For jumping upright, the **locust** has no rival, reaching a level equal to 35 times its height - this is like an athlete on a platform jumping up to the fifth floor of a building! The **Archer Fish** is the champion at shooting at a target. By shooting a jet of water from its mouth, it can catch insects up to a distance of 1.5 metres.*

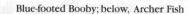
Blue-footed **Booby**; below, **Archer Fish**

The fastest...

On land, champions of speed are the **four-footed mammals**. Fastest of all is the **cheetah** which can reach speeds of 110 km/hr (kilometres per hour) - although it has to stop at least every 500 metres to get its breath back. Among its prey is the **Thompson Gazelle**, streaking across the Savannah, or African Bush, at 80 km/hr. From time to time gazelles may meet a herd of ferocious **buffalo** - but these are not so threatening as a lion which throws itself into the chase at a rate of almost 60 km/hr - a talented sprinter, despite its size.

Just as fast is the **American Antelope,** with an average speed of 50 -70 km/hr and unbeatable over medium to long distances. The **horse** and the **hyena** are both strong and fast, true champions in the 'middle distance' category. The **horse** gallops like the wind at over 60 km/hr, keeping the same pace up to 3000 - 4000 metres. The **hyena** proceeds more steadily, at 40 km/hr for at least 2000 - 3000 metres without being exhausted.

Many breeds of **dog** bred for racing are not all that far behind in the speed records. The **ostrich** is a special sort of 'sprinter'. It is two-legged, like all birds, but it does not fly. Instead, it can run at the incredible rate of 50-70 km/hr for at least 30 - 40 minutes non-stop!

FACT

Animal marathon runner is the **wolf**. Although it usually goes along at a rate of 8 km/hr, when it is hunting in a pack, it can keep up a speed of 60 km/hr for at least 20 minutes!

Cheetah, ostrich and a Thompson's Gazelle, in pursuit of their prey.

Sprinters in the sea and on earth

In the water, the speed record is held by the **Sail Fish** which in a calm sea can reach a speed of 109 km/hr, equal to 100 metres per 3.3 seconds. The *tuna* also deserves a mention, breaking the waves at 80 km/hr, a speed not even beaten by a large cat! **Sun Spiders** are the fastest *invertebrates*. They can cover 100 metres in 24 seconds, sometimes slowing down a little, but hardly ever stopping at all.

The **American Cockroach** moves at a speed of 5.4 km/hr - not much, it seems, but this is equivalent to 50 times its size per second!

SPRINTERS IN THE AIR

The fastest animals on our planet are **birds**. *And the fastest of all is the* **Peregrine Falcon** *(shown right) which at top speed can reach 180 - 200 km/hr. But even a strange-looking bird like the* **crane** *(right, below) can maintain a 'cruising speed' of around 70 - 80 km/hr during migration, a speed unequalled by deer.*

The strongest

The strongest animals are also the largest, because of the astonishing mass of muscle which they have developed due to their enormous size. The **African Elephant** weighs 7 tonnes, the **Asian Elephant** 5 tonnes, and they can each move loads of more than one tonne. The massive shape of the **Marine Elephant** together with a weight of more than 3.5 tonnes makes it a powerful and strong champion in combat with its rivals.

Giant snakes are no less strong. The **Boa Constrictor** and the **Python** are each able to capture and to crush prey as large as an antelope.

Python

Frog

Boa Constrictor

FACT

In relation to its size, the power of the long hind legs of a *frog* is far greater than that of cycling champions. It seems a shame that with such strong legs for jumping and climbing, the frog prefers swimming in a pond and croaking by the light of the moon...

FLY-WEIGHTS...

*Even smaller animals can display special strengths. Most birds in the family of fruit-eating **finches** are no bigger than a sparrow, with an average weight of only 55 grams. But when a finch wants to crack a nut, it can use its beak to exert the pressure of a mallet - about 15 kilograms per square centimetre. A tiny **ant** can transport weights four times heavier than itself, lifting up weights two and a half times heavier than its own weight.*

How strong and powerful is the foot of an elephant?

African Elephant

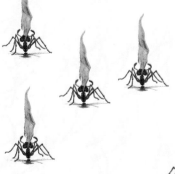

The most dangerous

The most dangerous animals are those which are *poisonous* - for instance, the small *Blue-Ringed Octopus*, the *Stone Fish*, the *Puffer Fish*, the *scorpion* and the deadly *Black Widow Spider*. Snakes such as the *Indian Cobra* and the *Australian Taipan* can cause the death of a person with one bite, which, in the case of the Taipan, contains a dose of poison powerful enough to kill 250,000 mice.

Many victims of the *Coral Snake* are small children, attracted by the bright colours of its spirals and its small size which makes it seem harmless.

In Central and South America live the most poisonous amphibians in the world, the *Arrow-Poison Frog* and the *Arrow-Poison Toad*. Native Indians rub up to 50 arrows on a live frog to poison their arrow-heads for hunting - one hundredth of a gram is enough to kill a person.

Another powerful animal is the *White Shark*, more than 12 metres long and weighing 3 tonnes. The double line of exceedingly sharp teeth (at least 3000) each one over 7 centimetres long and its incredibly strong jaw enables this ruthless predator to prey mainly on seals and dolphins. There are rarely more than 50 or 60 attacks on people reported each year throughout the world.

In the minds of both adults and children, the animals presumed to be the most dangerous are the *large predators*: *lions*, *leopards*, *buffalo*, *tigers*, *jaguars*. But a combination of needless hunting and a systematic destruction of their natural surroundings by human beings has reduced all these species dramatically. Each year, throughout the world, these so-called wild animals attack less victims than *jellyfish*, the common *bee* and smaller forms of animal life, such as the *Tsetse Fly* and the *Anopheles Mosquito* which carries malaria and which, in some tropical countries, causes over 3 million deaths each year.

Stone Fish

Jellyfish

Puffer Fish

FACT

Of all fish, the **Piranha** has the most voracious appetite. Even though it is small, just 30 - 60 centimetres at the most, a group of Piranha Fish can strip the flesh off large prey within a few seconds.

COLD SWEATS

*In some areas of Europe, there lives a species of black widow spider, known as the **Redback**. The female is just one centimetre long and has 13 red spots on her back. When she is annoyed, she may bite a person, causing sickness, fever, paralysis of the limbs and cold sweats - which is the first sign that the victim must see a doctor urgently.*

What jaws! These belong to the White Shark, the tiger and the cobra.

The largest

The largest animal of all is a marine mammal, the **Blue Whale**, which is over 30 metres in length and can weigh up to 200 tonnes - as much as 30 African Elephants! To satisfy its hunger, the Blue Whale eats between 200 - 300 kilograms of shrimps in one meal. With a maximum length of 18 metres, the **Whale Shark** is even as strong as an **elephant**, which is the largest and heaviest land mammal. An average elephant is 4 metres in height, over 7 tonnes in weight and to satisfy its enormous appetite, it eats about 250 kilograms of food per day and drinks 200 litres of water.

The **hippopotamus** and the **white rhinoceros** are heavyweights in the animal world, each with an average height of more than 1.5 metres and a weight of 3 - 4 tonnes. The rhinoceros can boast a horn of almost 1 metre in length.

Bisons, **buffalo** and **yak** each weigh on average about one tonne, plodding around the American prairies, the Indian plains and even above 5000 metres altitude in the Himalayan Mountains. The largest meat-eater is the **Brown Bear**, 3 metres in height and weighing 800 kilograms.

Another 'giant' is the **crocodile**, with an average length of 7 metres in length and 1 tonne in weight. And, perhaps just as ugly to look at, is the **Leatherback Sea Turtle**, weighing over 900 kilograms.

Crocodile

Huge and muscular: the Blue Whale, elephant, Brown Bear, buffalo, and the 'smallest' of these giants, the Komodo Dragon.

Hippopotamuses

SNAKES AND LIZARDS

The **Komodo Dragon** is the largest lizard in the world. An adult male can weigh up to 135 kilograms with a length of 3 metres. Among the snakes, both the **Python** and the **Anaconda** can be at least 10 metres long, but the **Anaconda** with its weight of 250 kilograms is the heaviest.

FACT

Among the primates (upright apes), the *gorilla* is the record-holder, 2 metres in height and over 200 kilograms in weight. A human being is sometimes referred to as 'the human ape' - but only a tall, heavy person can beat the gorilla in size!

▶ The largest

The **Goliath Frog**, an amphibian which lives in the African rivers, can reach exceptional dimensions - 3.5 kilograms in weight and 40 centimetres in length. Only the **American Bullfrog**, at 20 centimetres in length, comes anywhere near. However, the record among all amphibians goes to the **Giant Salamander** of Japan, 1.5 metres long!

Among the birds, undisputed champion is the **ostrich**, 2.7 metres tall and weighing 150 kilograms. Other giant birds can compete only in length. The **albatross** can boast a length of 1.35 metres and a wingspan of up to 3.5 metres - although its weight is no more than 10 kilograms, the same as that of a young woodpecker! In the Amazon Basin of South America there lives the largest beetle ever known - the **Hercules Beetle**. An adult Hercules Beetle is over 15 centimetres long, and one larva is longer than the palm of an adult hand!

The largest butterfly is the **Queen Alexandra Birdwing**, with a wingspan of at least 280 millimetres and a weight of 25 grams - a real giant!

The **Goliath Beetle** (shown in the picture) of the African equator is as large as a ripe apple - but this is small, compared to the 3.65 metres width between the front claws of the **Giant Crab**, as it moves around in the Japanese seas. Finally, we must not forget the **Giant Squid** (in the picture) which measures the same as a small fishing boat - over 20 metres.

FACT

The largest rodent is the **Capybara** or **Water Hog** which lives in South America. It is up to 1.5 metres long and weighs over 80 kilograms. Among the marsupials, the **Red Kangaroo** is a true heavyweight at 100 kilograms and measuring 2 metres tall.

Invertebrate Pachyderms

Among the invertebrates we find the pachyderms ('thick-skinned'). The *weta*, an insect from New Zealand and looking like an enormous cricket, weighs at least 70 grams. The **Emperor Scorpion** can reach a length of 18 centimetres and weighs over 50 grams. Among the invertebrate pachyderms are the gasteropods (broad-footed, one-piece shell). One notable gasteropod is the African **Giant Snail**, 100 centimetres long and weighing 900 grams.

GIGANTIC STARS!

The **Sea Star** *is a gigantic starfish. When its tentacles are fully extended, it can cover a surface of about one square metre - enough space to contain 100 of the more common, smaller starfish which live in the Mediterranean.*

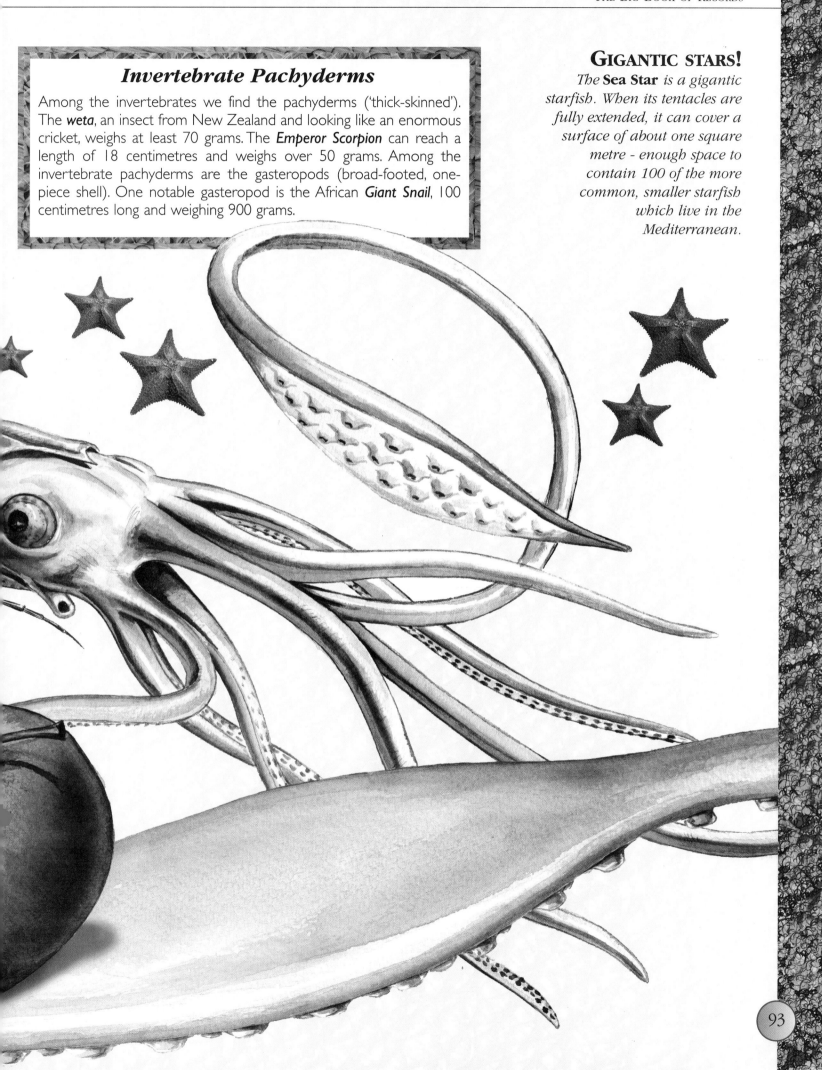

Dwarfs and...

The smallest land mammal is the **Etruscan Shrew**, about 6 centimetres long, including the tail, and weighing 2 grams at the most - about the same size as the world's smallest species of bird, the **hummingbird**, and at least 100 million times smaller than the Blue Whale.

The **Pygmy Bat** of Thailand is the lightest mammal that can fly, weighing less than 2 grams and no longer than 3.5 centimetres.

Among the smallest primates, the **Dwarf Lemur** (or Mouse Lemur) from Madagascar is about 6 centimetres long, plus a 14 centimetres long tail and weighs only 30 grams.

The smallest species of lizard is the **ghecko** which lives mainly in the warmer climates. So far, only 15 examples have been identified, the largest only 18 millimetres long.

The smallest fish on record is the **Sinarapan**, not more than 8.6 millimetres long and just 4 - 5 grams in weight. It is also the smallest known vertebrate.

The smallest amphibian is the **Cuban Tree Frog**, only between 8 - 12 millimetres long. The **Pencil Lead Snake** measures 10 millimetres at the most, small enough to go through the same hole as the lead of a pencil, hence its name.

Ticks and **mites** are the smallest arachnids and certainly among the most widespread. Their size can vary between one tenth of a millimetre and 3 centimetres.

Giraffe

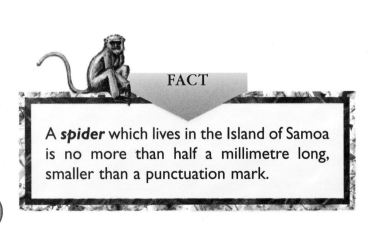

FACT

A **spider** which lives in the Island of Samoa is no more than half a millimetre long, smaller than a punctuation mark.

A hummingbird, dwarf lemur, shrew, ghecko, Cuban Tree Frog, all shorter than the first finger of a human. Put all together, they could comfortably fit into the palm of a hand.

...giants

The **giraffe** is the tallest animal in the world. The body of an adult male can reach a height of 5.5 metres, not counting the long neck. As well as being the largest animal on land, the **elephant** is also one of the tallest, with a height of 4 metres. And no other animal can match its huge ears! A special mention must also go to the **camel** and the **dromedary**, both weighing about 500 - 600 kilograms and looking down their noses at the world from a height of 2.2 - 3 metres.

African Elephant

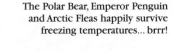

The strongest

The Polar Bear, Emperor Penguin and Arctic Fleas happily survive freezing temperatures... brrr!

The **Polar Bear** living in its snowy lair at the North Pole is certainly among the leaders when it comes to resistance to cold, surviving temperatures of minus 40˚C.

However, the **Emperor Penguin** at the South Pole withstands a climate which is even colder - minus 60˚C. The male Emperor Penguin keeps the one egg laid by the female under his feet, covering it with a fold of his skin and taking neither food nor drink for almost three months, until the egg is hatched.

In the scorching hot desert, the **dromedary**

(left) endures temperatures of 60 - 70˚C. It can go without eating or drinking for weeks, thanks to reserves of fat in its hump. When it comes to a well or an oasis, it 'fills up' with up to 140 litres of water in a little less than a quarter of an hour!

In the Australian desert, there lives a **frog** which is able to survive undisturbed for up to two years, waiting for the first rainfall to wake it up. Until then, as long as the drought lasts, the frog remains wrapped in its own warmth.

Walrus

FACT

The **Arctic Flea** is an insect just 2 millimetres long. It can face the harshest cold, with temperatures up to minus 15˚C, thanks to a natural antifreeze substance produced by its body.

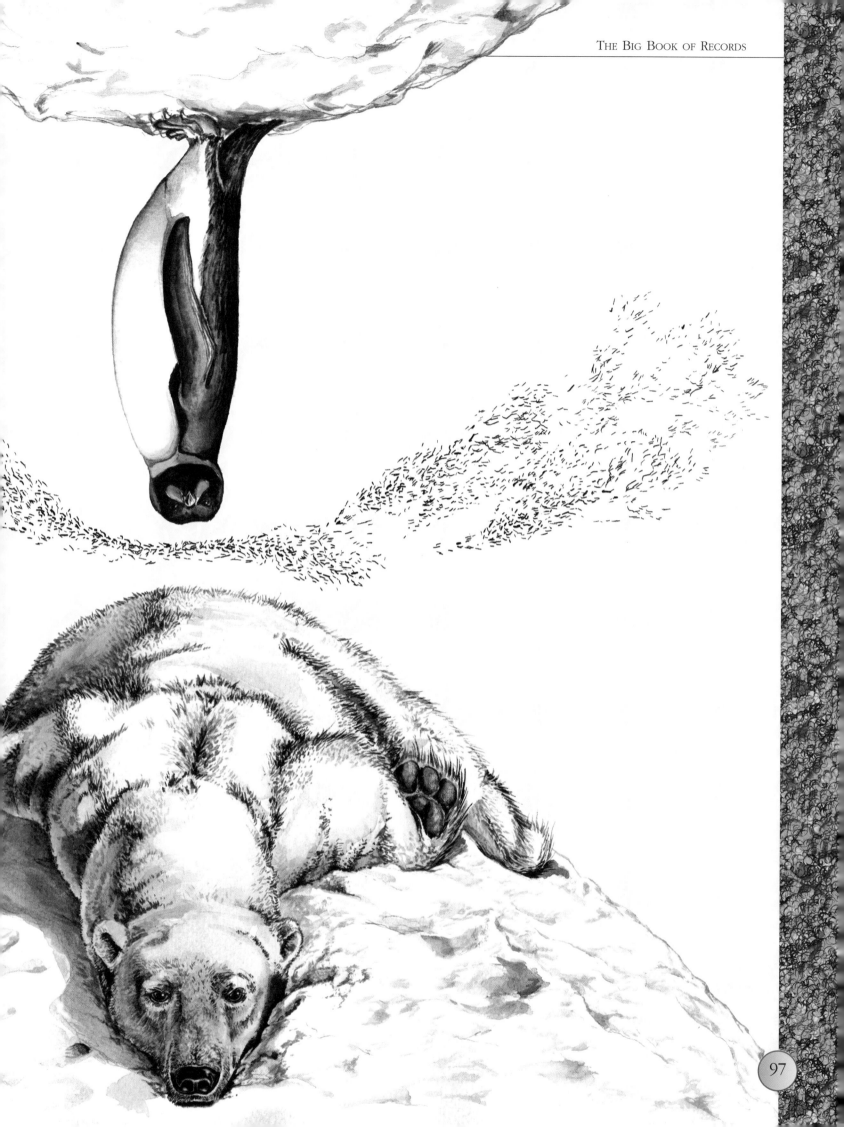

Breathing records

A marine mammal, the **sperm whale** holds the record for staying underwater. It can stay at a depth of 1000 metres for an hour without needing to take a breath. The **Emperor Penguin** is also a skilled underwater swimmer. In the icy Ross Sea of the Antarctic it can dive to a depth of up to 400 - 500 metres, remaining underwater for up to twenty minutes.

FLYING MAMMALS

The largest flying mammals in the world are **Flying Foxes**. *These are actually bats, measuring 45 centimetres long, weighing 1.5 kilograms and with a wingspan of 1.7 metres.*

Sperm Whale

Arctic Tern

Long distance champions

During migration, the Arctic Tern can cover thousands and thousands of kilometres within a few weeks. It flies up to 160 kilometres per day, according to the direction of the wind - a total of 36,000 kilometres east across the continents, then across the oceans of the southern hemisphere and on to the South Pole.

Champion of non-stop flight is the **New Zealand Cuckoo** which arrives at the Solomon Isles in the Pacific after an uninterrupted journey of 440 kilometres without food.

Wild swans can fly at a height equal to that of Mount Everest.

Flying at height

The record for flying at the greatest height goes to the **Griffon Vulture** *(some examples being quoted are for more than 11,000 metres) and* **wild swans** *which fly along the route of airlines at a height of 8000 metres.*

FACT

The **Black Tern** can remain in flight up to ten years without ever perching - eating, sleeping and mating in the air!

Griffon Vulture

Great travellers

The **gnu** is one of the most tireless of travellers. Between the dry and the rainy season each year it has to travel in search of food and water, crossing the plains and the African savannah of Serengeti, across Tanzania and Kenya, following a course of hundreds of kilometres. It is a very dangerous journey, not only because of the large predators such as lions and tigers, and the crocodiles which infest the rivers, but also because of hunters.
The North-American reindeer, the **caribou**, (shown in the picture) undertake a journey of at least 3000 kilometres during the course of

their seasonal migration from the Arctic tundra to the forests of the Canadian taiga.
The **lemming** (in the picture) is a small Arctic rodent. On average, the population of a lemming colony increases up to 200 times every four years. That means that some lemmings must leave in search of new territories, journeying thousands of kilometres. Migration often ends tragically, with the death of thousands of lemmings falling into the waters of the seas and oceans.

GREAT NAVIGATORS

Eels *are the great explorers of the animal world. From the Sargasso Sea in the Atlantic Ocean, they swim to the European coastline. From there, each adult eel must return to the Sargasso Sea to spawn, swimming thousands and thousands of kilometres across the sea.*

For a journey in the opposite direction, the champion is the **salmon***. From a river, it swims out to sea, swimming thousands of kilometres. Then, like a pilgrim, it returns to its original home, rising with the currents and the torrents, guided by instinct and by the scents of a particular course of water.*

The **Sea Turtle** *is a true 'sea wanderer', going out from the beach where it is born within a range of at least 1500 kilometres, swimming, if necessary, 40 kilometres each day on average.*

Top left, eel. Above, Sea Turtle

The longest living

Although it is true that **turtles** are among the longest-lived animals, the **Galápagos Tortoise** lives more than 150 years. The **Tuatara**, a species of reptile dating back 220 million years is almost extinct, but it can live more than 100 years. The **Quahog**, a species of giant clam living in tropical seas can survive for 200 years!

The largest living mollusc, the **Giant Clam**, with the two halves of its shell each measuring up to 135 centimetres and weighing 350 kilograms, easily survives to 100 years, also the **Spiny Lobster**. We know of eels living more than 80 years, and which still fling themselves about with the energy of young fish. Whilst some **sturgeons** live up to 180 years, **goldfish** can live to 40 years, as long as the water in their aquarium is changed frequently.

Most people think of the **parrot** as being long-lived. In fact, a parrot rarely lives much beyond 30 years - although there are some **cockatoos** which can survive more than 80 years. The **Californian Condor** (photograph above) can live as long - but it is in danger of extinction. In 1995, there were only 104 of these birds.

Spiny Lobster

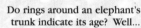
Do rings around an elephant's trunk indicate its age? Well...

Parrot

FACT

The pupa of a **Mayfly** can remain for up to 2 -3 years on a water lily, on the surface of a swamp, lake or stream. But when the adult finally emerges, it may live only for one hour, just time to flap its wings!

Giant Clam

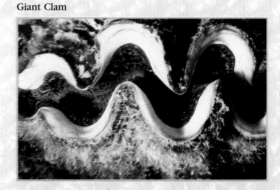

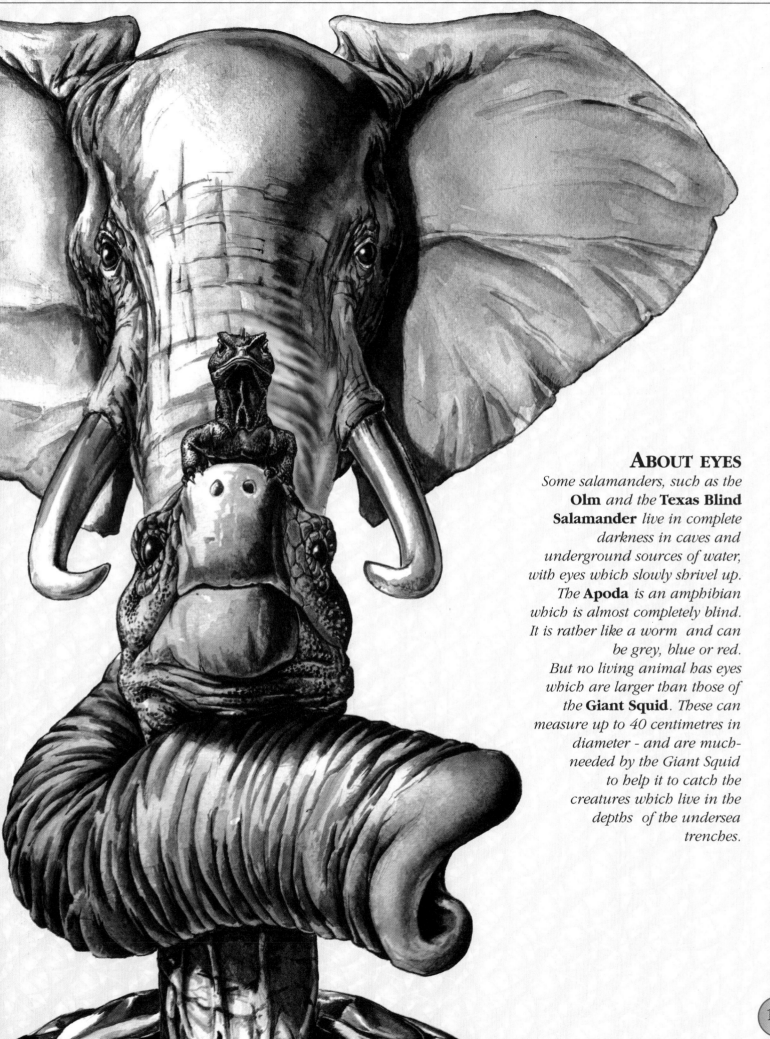

ABOUT EYES

Some salamanders, such as the **Olm** and the **Texas Blind Salamander** live in complete darkness in caves and underground sources of water, with eyes which slowly shrivel up. The **Apoda** is an amphibian which is almost completely blind. It is rather like a worm and can be grey, blue or red. But no living animal has eyes which are larger than those of the **Giant Squid**. These can measure up to 40 centimetres in diameter - and are much-needed by the Giant Squid to help it to catch the creatures which live in the depths of the undersea trenches.

Remarkable birds

The **Wandering Albatross** is up to 135 centimetres long, and is the bird with the largest wingspan - over 3 metres! The longest beak, almost half a metre, belongs to the **Pelican**, which it also uses as an efficient fishing hook! The beak of the **Sword-Billed Hummingbird** measures over half its body length of 25 centimetres, including its tail. The **ostrich**, as well as being the largest bird in the world, is also the bird which lays the largest egg - 24 times larger than the egg of a chicken. The shell has a thickness of 1.5 millimetres, and can support the weight of an adult person. The smallest egg belongs to the **Vervain Hummingbird** of Jamaica (shown in the large picture), one tenth of a millimetre in length, and weighing just 0.365 grams. When it comes to talking, the African **Grey Parrot** is a true champion - a vocabulary of 800 words is nothing remarkable! The **chicken** is the

bird which is most widespread. It is estimated that in the world there are ten million at any one time. One variety, the **Long-Necked Chicken** or **Japanese Yokohama** has the longest feathers in the world - its tail feathers are more than 10 metres long.

North American Eagle on its nest

Pelicans

FACT

The nest of an **eagle** is the largest in the world - 3 metres wide, 6 metres deep and up to 2 tonnes in weight. Even eagle chicks help with the building!

Strange animals!

The **mayfly** is one of the earliest winged insects. The adult lives for only a few hours, during which time it must reproduce, in order for the species to survive.

A colony of **termites** construct the largest insect nest in the world, 10 - 12 metres in height and in the form of a tower. **Prairie Dogs**, small North American mammals, dig underground tunnels up to 30 metres long in which thousands of individuals can live. The female **Golden Orbita Spider** is up to 100 times larger than her companion - the male is so small, it is not even worth eating! The two most timid of animals are the **Giant Panda** and the rarest of monkeys, the **Golden Tamarin** from Brazil - no human being ever gets very close to this animal.

The **Duck-Billed Platypus** is a strange animal which has the bill of a duck, the skeleton of a reptile and lays eggs like birds and reptiles. But because it feeds its young with its own milk, it is classified as a mammal. **Sponges** were believed to be plants for a long time. Instead, they are animals with at least 5000 different species. The **locust** is not the only creature which causes destruction by its greediness. The **African Snail** devours plant-life at such a rate that when it attacks crops, it usually causes a real disaster. At 30 centimetres long, it is also the largest snail in the world.

Top and centre, varieties of sponges.
Below, Koala.
Bottom left; Duck-Billed Platypus

FACT

The Australian **koala** is very fussy and eats almost exclusively a particular type of eucalyptus leaves; in order to get its daily ration of 500 grams, it has to strip ten trees, ignoring enormous quantities of other food.

The **Roadrunner** is a strange bird which rarely flies, preferring to run along on the ground on its strong 'paws' at a remarkable speed of 32 km/hr. And although the kangaroo may not be able to walk, it can cover a distance of 12 metres with just one jump - more than four estate cars, laid end to end. The **dolphin** is regarded as one of the most intelligent animals. Among the invertebrates, the **common octopus** is also highly intelligent. The **dormouse** spends nine months of the year sleeping so deeply that even if it falls out of its nest, it does not wake up.

High on the list of the most annoying animals must be the **Howler Monkey** from Central America. Its cries are so sharp and so penetrating that they can be heard up to 4 kilometres away. **Sharks** also like making sounds. They send their 'messages' by infra-sound (soundwaves lower than those normally received by the human ear). These can reach up to 180 decibels and cover an area of 120 kilometres. The tiny **American Fieldmouse** can produce up to 17 litters in one season - at least 150 babies. But the **Horse Fly** is even more fertile, producing a family of millions in just one year. Despite its name, a **stick insect** lays a gigantic egg, similar in size to a small nut.

Top, Giant Panda; Central, Howler Monkey, Bottom, shrew; Bottom of page, two dolphins

RECORD NEWS
ANIMALS

To be or not to be...

From the beginnings of the first forms of life on Earth, 2.5 billion years ago, there have been at least five mass extinctions. There are many theories as to the cause of the sudden disappearance of many species, happening at the same time. Palaeontologists (scientists who study fossils of animals from prehistoric times) believe there could be many reasons - variations in climate, sudden changes in the environment, geographical changes in the structure of Earth's crust, and natural disasters, such as enormous volcanic eruptions or the fall of gigantic meteorites.

The most famous mass extinction is the one which took place at the end of the **Mesozoic Era**, between 70 and 65 million years ago, with the complete disappearance of the dinosaurs, flying and marine reptiles, plus many species of invertebrates which lived in water - such as ammonites, whose tiny fossilized shells we can often find in some chalky rocks. During this time, it is calculated that from 50% to 70% of species then living were lost forever. Before this, other large extinctions had threatened life on Earth.

During the **Ordovician Period**, between 500 and 470 million years ago, because of great fluctuations in the levels of the seas, about 85% of marine species which then existed, including many brachiopods (tiny organisms similar to molluscs) disappeared for ever.

In the **Devonian Period** (about 360-350 million years ago), 83% of the most ancient species of fish, the placoderms, fearful predators of the oceans with their strong jaws, were wiped out because of a sudden cooling-down of the planet. It is believed that the impact of giant meteorites caused a sharp decrease in the volume of oxygen in the seas.

The most notable extinction in the **Permian Age**, 250 million years ago, was of the dominant species of the seas. These were the tribolites, animals with a hard upper shell and ancestor of the arthropods. During this time, 95% of marine species disappeared. This was because of the violent variations in climate and the levels of the oceans, intense volcanic activity, and, probably, also by a shower of comets and asteroids which hit the Earth.

We end with the **Triassic Age**, 200 million years ago, when again 80% of the marine species then living disappeared. It is believed that this was due to volcanic eruptions of such power that the result was a sharp increase in the climate of Earth and the waters of the oceans.

In our modern times, many biologists, zoologists and entomologists have voiced their fears about the possibility of further mass extinctions. It is estimated that some species of animals are disappearing at a rate of 10,000 times more than the natural rate of extinction. During the last hundred years, 95% of the total tiger population, plus 10-12 million elephants, have disappeared, either captured or killed by humans.

WORLD RECORDS
PLANTS
and
TREES

Woods and forests

Over half the total number of animals and plants on our planet live in the ***tropical rain forests*** which extend across the equatorial zones. Here, there can be up to 400 animals in just one tree! The ***Amazon rain forest*** is the largest tropical forest in the world, but the largest ***forest of conifer and birch trees*** is the ***Siberian Taiga***. Suriname is the country with the largest surface covered by forest – 91% of the entire land, followed by the Solomon Islands with 89%, then Papua New Guinea with 83%.

The prairies are vast stretches of different types of grasses, but few trees. The largest prairies in the world, each quite different to the others in terms of their natural surroundings, are the ***African Savannah*** (or African bush), the ***Argentinian Pampas*** and the ***Euroasian Steppes***.

Botanists have classified about 380,000 different species of plant-life. The highest number of plants belong to the group called ***angiosperms*** (flowering plants), with over 250,000 species, all reproducing by the seeds produced within their flowers.

Among the flowering plants, the largest family is that of the ***orchids***, with over 35,000 species. We know of at least 500 species of ***meat-eating plants***.

There are also about 10,000 different species of ***ferns***, 12,000 species of ***algae*** and 100,000 varieties of ***fungi***. In one square hectare of rain forest it is possible to find up to 200 different species of plant-life.

Siberian Taiga

FACT

The largest number of rings ever counted in a tree is 280 for each centimetre of rays in its trunk. The tree was a ***Sequoia*** at least 4000 years old. The most rapidly growing plant is believed to be a ***False Acacia*** in Malaya - a growth of 10 metres in less than a year. But even this is nothing, compared to some species of ***bamboo*** which can grow an outstanding 90 centimetres in one day!

Argentinian Pampas

The Puffball is a gigantic fungus, large enough to be noticed even with taller plants nearby...

Top: in the Amazon rain forest

Centre: orchids

Bottom: a meat-eating plant

Trees and... tree trunks

The oldest species of tree is the **Ginkgo Biloba** which originated in China about 160 million years ago. Other living 'ancients' are the **horsetails**, **mosses** and **ferns**, all of which were flourishing on Earth at the time of the dinosaurs. The **Eternal God**, a Californian Sequoia 12,000 years old, was growing before the construction of the pyramids in Ancient Egypt, and is the oldest tree that we know - 72 metres tall and with a diameter of 6 metres. The **sequoias** are the longest-lived trees, with an average life of 2200 - 3000 years. The largest tree in the world is the *General Sherman* in the *Sequoia National Park* in California, US. Its trunk has a diameter of 11 metres, it is 83 metres tall, and is believed to be more than 2200 years old. With its wood it would be possible to make 600,000 floorboards, at least 115 houses, 5 billion safety matches and as many cocktail sticks as there are people in the world... at an estimated weight of 1400 tonnes, equal to 25 articulated lorries, it must be the heaviest living plant on Earth!

The **Giant Eucalyptus** tree which grows in South Australia beats this for height - about 90 metres tall! - and the largest fruits also belong to another species of eucalyptus, the *Silverleaf Eucalyptus*. The tallest tree of all is the *Medicine Tree*, an American sequoia with a height of 117 metres, high enough to compete with the Statue of Liberty...

FACT

The record for the widest tree trunk, which can be from 10 to 40 metres in circumference, belongs to the African **Baobob**, which can reach the size of an enormous umbrella of 80 metres.

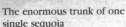
The enormous trunk of one single sequoia

The tallest tree of all, the Medicine Tree, reaches up to the sky, high above the torch of the Statue of Liberty.

Gingko biloba

Water Hyacinth

Baobab

Sequoia

DANGEROUS PLANTS!

*The stinging leaves of the **Ulmaceae Nettle** from New Zealand contains deadly poisons. Just one touch can cause the death of many animals, including dogs and horses. No plant causes more damage to crops than the weed **Sow Thistle**, but the **Water Hyacinth** causes more infestation on water. Although this is a small plant, it reproduces so rapidly that it can soon cover long tracts of rivers or the entire surface of a pond, so that boats cannot get through. The **Strangler Fig** is a parasitic plant which grows in tropical forests. Very, very slowly, it clings to the host plant, gradually taking its light, water and nutriments, until the Strangler Fig causes the death of the host plant. Then, with its typical hollow trunk, it grows triumphantly towards the sky. The **Japanese Knotweed** is the fastest-growing 'super-weed', growing 10cm in a single day and with roots going 3 metres deep into the soil.*

113

▶ More trees and trunks

One example of the **Montezuma Cypress** tree from Mexico is more than 40 metres tall and boasts a gigantic trunk of over 36 metres in circumference.

The **Banyan Fig** or Banyan Tree, (see picture) is widespread in tropical areas, and is about 30 metres in height. No other tree extends across such a wide area. This is because of the many aerial roots which descend from its branches towards the ground, where they are 'transformed' into tree trunks. These, in turn, give support to the tree, enabling it to spread over a vast surface. In the Calcutta Botanical Gardens in India grows the largest Banyan Tree in the world: it leans on more than 1000 trunks and covers an area of 16,000 square metres, as large as an enormous car park with space for more than 4000 cars. The tree with the smallest trunk is probably the Canadian **White Cedar**, only 10 centimetres high and which can live more than 150 years.

But in the Arctic, it is the tiny **White Willow** which lives the longest - its size enables it to withstand the freezing winds of the far north.

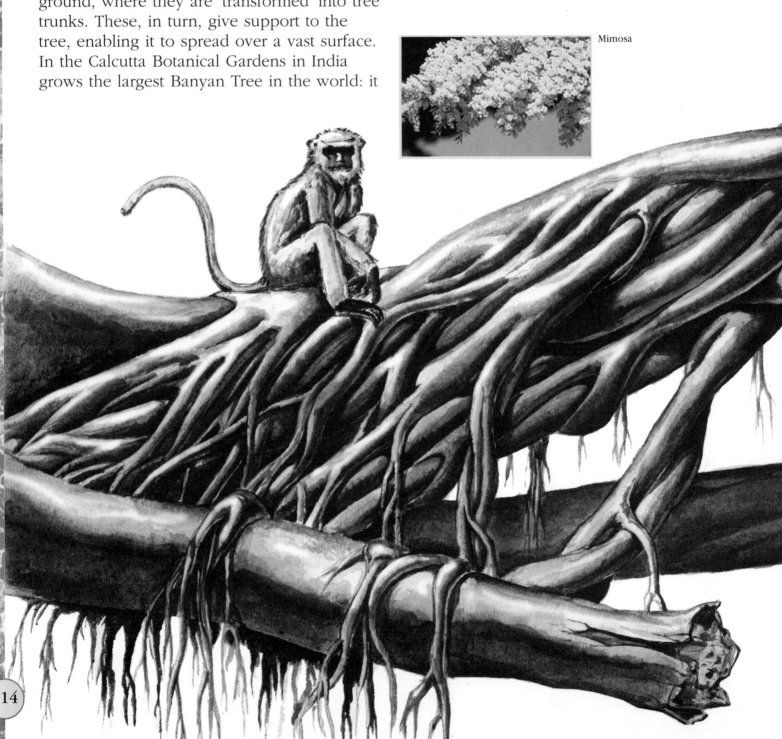

Mimosa

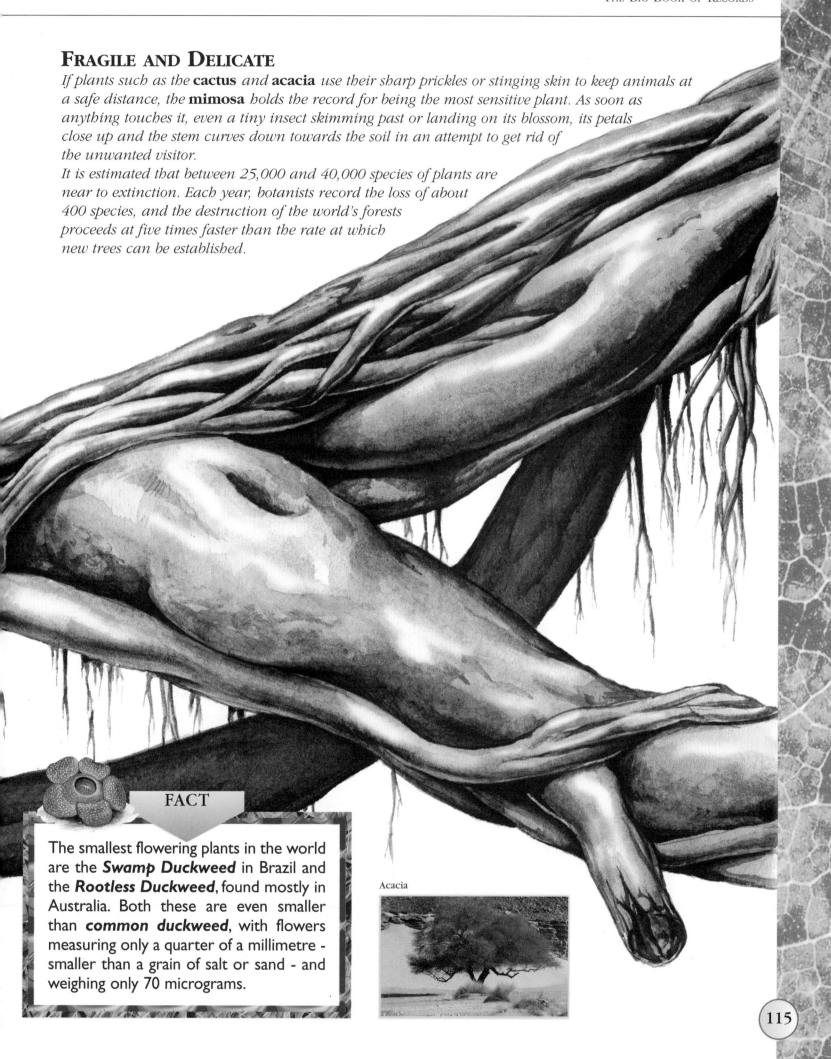

FRAGILE AND DELICATE

If plants such as the **cactus** *and* **acacia** *use their sharp prickles or stinging skin to keep animals at a safe distance, the* **mimosa** *holds the record for being the most sensitive plant. As soon as anything touches it, even a tiny insect skimming past or landing on its blossom, its petals close up and the stem curves down towards the soil in an attempt to get rid of the unwanted visitor.*

It is estimated that between 25,000 and 40,000 species of plants are near to extinction. Each year, botanists record the loss of about 400 species, and the destruction of the world's forests proceeds at five times faster than the rate at which new trees can be established.

FACT

The smallest flowering plants in the world are the *Swamp Duckweed* in Brazil and the *Rootless Duckweed*, found mostly in Australia. Both these are even smaller than **common duckweed**, with flowers measuring only a quarter of a millimetre - smaller than a grain of salt or sand - and weighing only 70 micrograms.

Acacia

Leaves

The **Raffia Palm** is a plant native to Madagascar. One leaf can grow to a length of 20 metres, the smallest 4 metres. The leaves of the **Bamboo Palm** from the Amazon are just as big. These are the trees with the largest leaves in the world.
The leaves of the **Agave** reach 2 metres in length, and its flowers can also be up to 10 metres high.

Leaves of the Agave

Flowers of the Agave

Roots

The deepest roots belong to the **Transvaal Wild Fig** in South Africa, which can go down 120 metres into the ground: the plant with the longest roots is **wild rye** which, incredibly, can grow over 620 kilometres of roots in just 5 square centimetres of earth. The **Mangrove** grows in tropical surroundings, in the salty waters of swamps and marshes and at the mouth of large rivers. Its roots are like a mesh of tall poles and these form huge arches which anchor the plant to its muddy bed.

FACT

In just one 'picking', a 212 year-old Portuguese **Cork Oak** produced a quantity of cork sufficient to make at least 100,000 stoppers for bottles (see picture).

Aquatic plants

The tallest-growing aquatic plant is the Papyrus. Its trunk can reach a height of 5 metres. The largest is a gigantic water lily, the Queen Victoria (Victoria Regia) which grows in tropical forests. Its leaves can grow more than 2 metres in diameter. The smallest water plants are the duckweed family.

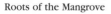

Roots of the Mangrove

Papyrus

Herbaceous plants

There are at least 7500 species of herbaceous plants (plants without woody trunks and which die off in winter) widespread throughout almost all regions of the world. The largest herbaceous plant in the world is the Giant Ambrosia which can reach a height of 3.65 metres, with leaves 90 centimetres long. It grows throughout America.

duckweed

Queen Victoria
(Victoria Regia)

Flowers

The **magnolia** (see picture) is one of the most ancient species of flowers, flourishing 90 million years ago, more or less 25 million years before the disappearance of the dinosaurs.

The **sunflower** may appear to be one large flower - but its corolla (or crown) is made up of lots of tiny flowers. A sunflower can grow to 8 metres tall, and the corolla can measure up to 80 centimetres in diameter.

But the record for the most unusual plant must go to the rare **Giant Bromeliad** of South America. This is the largest plant on our planet, about 10 metres in height, and which produces a spectacular abundance of flowers of at least 8000 pure white blooms in the course of just one flowering. This happens at the end of its life, which can last between 80 and 150 years.

The strongest smelling flower is the **Amorphophallus Titanum**, over 2 metres in height, and often called the Stinking Lily. Its flowers give off the smell of rotten meat to within a range of 800 metres.

Birch blossom

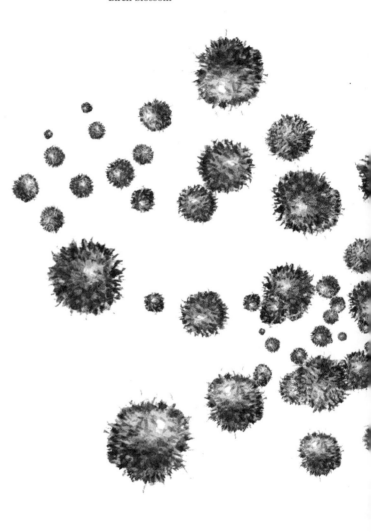

FACT

The largest flower in the world (and also one which gives off a smell of rotting meat) is the **Rafflesia Arnoldi** which grows in the tropical rain forests. Not counting the stem or the leaves, it can measure up to 1 metre in diameter and weigh between 7 and 10 kilograms.

Sunflowers

Flocks of cotton

Just one handful of cotton wool...
One handful of cotton, only as large as a golf ball, can contain up to 500 thousand cotton fibres with lots of seeds…

POLLEN

Flowers carry out the important task of producing the seeds which will generate new plants. Pollen is produced by the stamens, the male part of a plant. Even the largest grain of pollen has a diameter of only 0.2 millimetres, smaller than a punctuation mark. One birch blossom can produce up to 5.5 million grains of pollen.

Seeds and fruits

In its natural state, the **Evening Primrose** grows in the North American Desert. This plant has developed an ingenious system to enable its seeds to travel for kilometres along the sand dunes, searching for ideal conditions to take root. It is like the **Alstroemeria**, a climbing plant which grows in the Asiatic tropical forests. Each seed has a little 'wing', only one fifteenth of a centimetre long, and this enables the seed to fly like a tiny aeroplane before finding the right sort of ground to take root.

The **Sycamore** tree produces 'flying fruit' which twirl through the air like the blades of a helicopter.

A **coconut** can weigh up to 18 kilograms and so it is one of the largest seeds. Because of the vegetable fibre covering it, the coconut can travel for miles on water, floating on the waves, and taking root up to 10 years later on beaches and islands thousands of kilometres away.

The **Epiphytic Orchid** produces microscopic seeds - one thousand seeds weigh barely one gram! But as for large petals, nothing in the plant world can beat the **Jacob's Ladder Orchid** - 90 centimetres long. The **pumpkin** is a fruit which can reach gigantic dimensions, up to 400 kilograms in weight!

coconuts

FACT

The largest nut in the world is the **Coco de Mer** on the Seychelles in the Indian Ocean. This heart-shaped nut can weigh more than 18 kilograms and take up to 6 years to reach maturity!

Sycamore tree

Bread from Trees

The *Breadfruit Tree* which grows in Central Asia, produces the largest fruit in the world, each one weighing up to 30 kilograms - the weight of a 6 or 7 year-old child.

The fruit of the *Baobab*, also called the 'Monkey Bread' tree, is among the most unusual. Each one is about 30 centimetres long and hangs from the tree on a stem rather like a rope.

Plant and the fruit of the Breadfruit Tree

121

Plants of the desert

The **Giant Saguaro** is a cactus which grows in the deserts of Arizona, in the USA and in Mexico. It can grow up to 15 metres tall and with spines 7 centimetres long. It weighs up to 8 - 9 tonnes and can live up to 200 years. When it rains, the plant can absorb enough water in its trunk to increase its size by 50% - that is, enough water to fill at least 100 bath-tubs.

In the Australian desert we find the most gaudy flowers of the dry zone - the **Clianthus** or **The Sturt's Desert Pea**, brilliant red in colour.

The **Lithops** originally came from the South African desert, where it still grows in the wild. It is often called the 'Stone Plant' or 'Living Stone'. The plant has no stem, just two leaves which develop under the ground, until the tips can be seen. These tips become round and flat with a slit across the top, looking just like stones on the ground.

Amanita Phalloides   Clianthus

Lithops

FUNGHI

The largest mushroom in the world is the **Giant Vescia**, *similar to the enormous basket of an air balloon - it can measure up to one metre in diameter and weigh up to 18 kilograms. The oldest and most extensive fungus is an* **Armillaria Ostoyae**, *2400 years old and which extends in the subsoil of a forest in the state of Washington, USA, for 890 hectares - an area equal to 1220 football pitches. In the Philippines there grows a species of fungus which gives off a green light up to a distance of 30 metres. But the most poisonous fungus is the* **Amanita Phalloides**. *50 grams is sufficient to cause the death of an adult person.*

FERNS, ALGAE AND LICHENS

Algae produce 70% of the oxygen needed by all living things on our planet. The algae which is the longest in the world is the **Macrocystis Pyrifera**, which is a species of brown algae, or kelp. This grows in the Pacific Ocean, at least 45 centimetres each day, and can reach up to 60 metres in length.
Lichens are very strong plants which can resist temperatures from the very high to the very low. Some species are widespread throughout the Antarctic and these can withstand temperatures of minus 20°C.
Tree ferns are gigantic plants which grow in tropical regions, reaching a height of almost 20 metres.

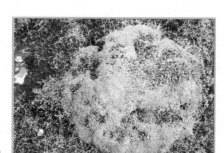

Lichen

Lichen

Welwitschia

Tree ferns

FACT

In the deserts of South West Africa grows the *Welwitschia*, a plant which can live 2000 years. It has only two ribbon-like leaves which grow and then extend along the ground up to a distance of 3 metres.

RECORD NEWS
PLANTS
and
TREES

The invasion of the mahogany pirates

Wood from the *Mahogany* tree has been widely used in the manufacture of quality furniture for hundreds of years. Now it is so rare that helicopters survey great tracts of the Amazon rain forest to discover the few surviving trees. At first sight of a mahogany tree, a team of wood-cutters begin destroying many square kilometres of growing plants in order to obtain just one of the last examples of this precious wood. Wood-cutters may get 30 dollars per trunk. Its commercial value is up to 80,000 dollars. The situation regarding the state of the world's rain forests is serious. Already 80% of the total area of forest has been destroyed. Now, there are 3870 million hectares to save from systematic destruction. Botanists and scientists are constantly reporting that a large part of the 'green lungs' of the Earth is at risk of disappearing within the next 50 years. Throughout the world, 140,000 square kilometres of forest, an area equal to a football pitch, is cut down every two seconds throughout every year. Within the last 30 years in Brazil, an area as large as France, 55 million hectares, has been destroyed - that is 58% of the Amazon rain forest, lost for ever. In Indonesia 70% of wood has been cut down and exported illegally, whilst in Central Africa and in the basin of the River Congo, over two thirds of the original tropical forest has been lost. This is one of the deprived regions in the world, but the destruction of the rain forest does nothing to improve the lives of the people or their surroundings.

In Russia, 1500 hectares of conifers vanish each year, whilst in the USA 94% of its major forests has been razed to the ground. In Canada, only 400 million hectares of forest remain, but with a flourishing industry in wood.

In most of South America, there is a constant drive to find areas for cattle-rearing to meet the demand of world markets by cheap, intensive farming methods. This, in turn, attracts thousands of people living below poverty level, so the forest regions have to make way for new farming areas. More of the forest disappears, and with it the disappearance of many other species of animals - leopards, bears, musk deer, Siberian tigers, orang-utans and whole colonies of tropical birds.

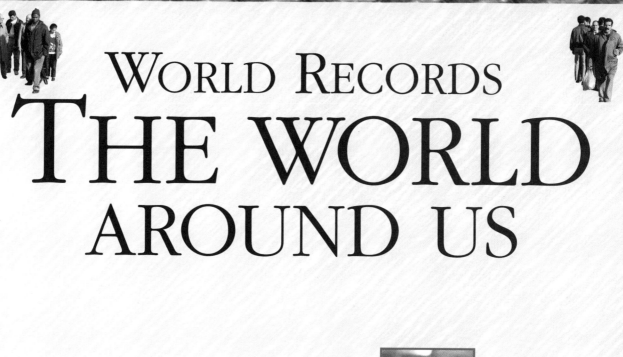

World Records
THE WORLD
AROUND US

The countries of the world

There are 192 countries in the world. The smallest is **Vatican City**, with an area of less than 0.5 sq. km., equal to one hundred football pitches. The largest country is **Russia** - 17,070.289 sq. km (42 million times bigger than Vatican City). The next largest is **Canada** 9,970,537 sq. km. in size, followed by **China**, 9,596,961 sq. km. and the **United States**, 9,372,614 sq. km. At the other end of the scale are small countries such as **Liechtenstein**, with a total area of 160 sq. km., the Polynesian (Pacific) islands of **Tuvalu**

(25.9 sq. km.) and **Nauru** (21 sq. km.) and the tiny European pricipality of **Monaco** (1.8 sq. km.). **China** has the most extensive borders in the world (22,143 km.) and also the highest number of neighbouring countries (16) followed by **Russia** with 20,139 km. and 14 neighbouring sovereign states. The longest line of demarcation (established boundary) between two countries is that which separates the **United States** and **Canada** - 243,791 km., which is five times more extensive than those of the Indonesian island group of 54,716 km.

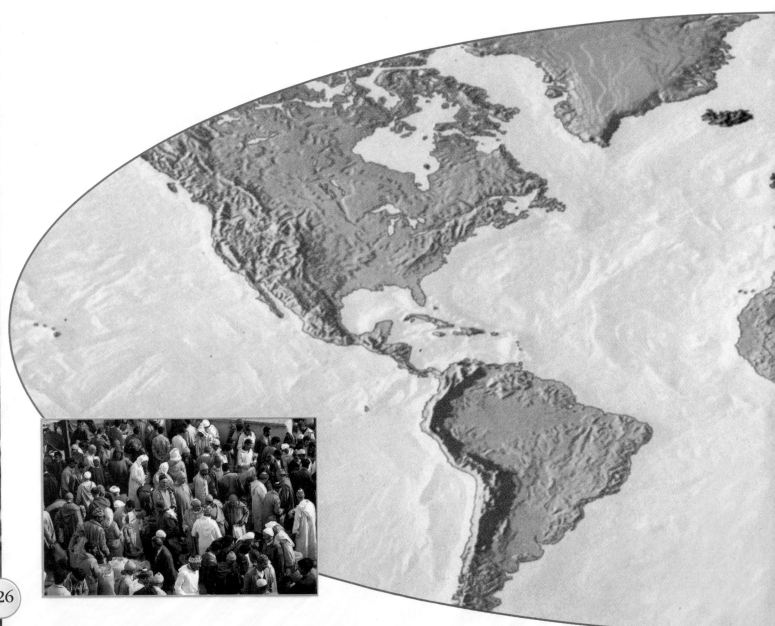

Chinese people (above) and Indian people (below) travelling by public transport.
Bottom corner, left-hand page, an Arab market-place.

CITIES OF THE WORLD

The population of the entire world is estimated at 5,951,400,000. The most heavily populated country is **China** *with 1,250,000,000 inhabitants, followed by India, with 998,000,0000. Together, these two countries constitute more than one third of the world's population -* **India** *alone has a population three times larger than that of the* **United States**, *and is the third most heavily-populated country with a population of 276,000,000.*
The 'micro-states' of **Nauru** *and* **Tuvalu** *in the Pacific Ocean, each have a little less than 10,000 inhabitants.*
Vatican City *is the least-populated country in the world.*
There are 23 countries with an estimated total of 50,000,000 cities, and 14 countries with an estimated total of less than 100,000 cities.

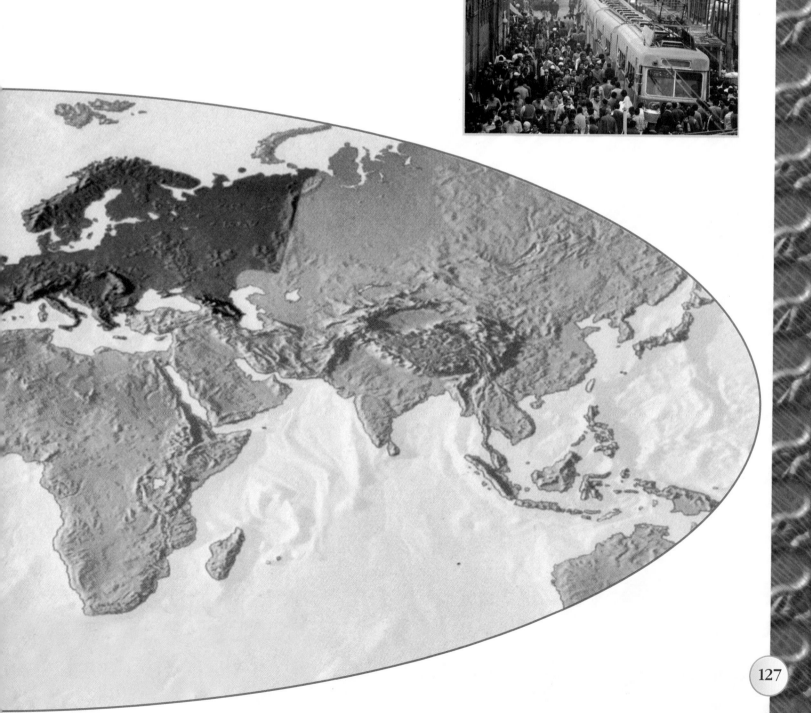

Work and development

Oil refinery in Kuwait

When people talk about 'the workforce' they refer to those people who are employed in the different processes of making goods and providing services. In **Kuwait** an estimated 64.6% of the population are employed and so make up the workforce. In **Singapore**, it is 58%. By contrast, in **Armenia** only 36.4% of people are employed in work. In **Columbia** the percentage is only 17%. In general, we can say that the countries which are most developed benefit by having the most industry and a high growth of technology. The most developed countries have 20% of the world population. They possess 80% of the world's wealth and use 70% of resources and energy. The under-developed countries of the Third World (most of Latin America and a large number of African and Asian states) have 80% of the total world population. Yet they have only 20% of the world's wealth and use only 30% of global energy.

An Iraqi peasant sifting grain

A WANDER AROUND THE WORLD

The countries visited by the largest number of tourists are - first, **France** *with an annual total of 73,042,000 visitors, then* **Spain** *with 51,772,000, the* **United States** *with 48,491,000 and in fourth place,* **Italy***, with 36,097,000 tourists.*

Refinery

Trinità dei Monti, Rome

The pyramid at the Louvre Museum, Paris

The Mosque at Cordoba, Spain

Manhattan Bridge, New York

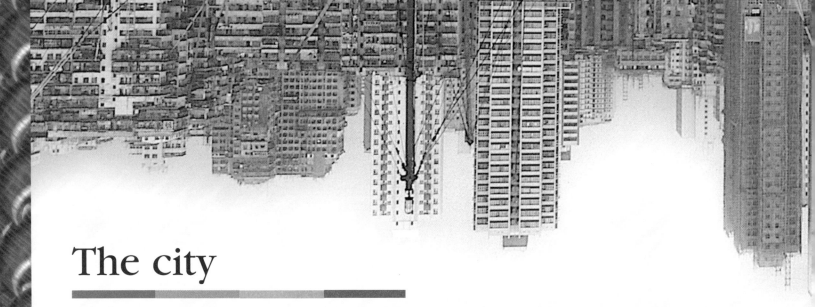

The city

According to statistics, in the course of a little more than ten years, half the world's population will live in cities. Urbanization (the spread of city development) is most rapid in the Third World, where within the last 50 years the population living in city areas has reached 39% of the total population. Today in the world there are 41 cities with five million or more inhabitants. By the year 2015, there will be over 23 million and almost all countries will be in the process of development.

Hong Kong is the most densely populated city in the world, with 98,000 inhabitants per sq. km., followed by *Lagos* in Nigeria with 67,000 inhabitants per sq. km. *Mumbai* (Bombay) in India is one of the largest cities on Earth, and at the same time, one of the most densely populated with 55,000 people per sq. km. It also has a high cost of living, about 20 times above that of European cities such as *Paris*, *London* or *Rome*.

Capital cities are generally the largest, most heavily populated and important in a country. Sometimes, the city with the largest number of inhabitants is one of the major centres, but not the capital. *Shanghai*, in China, for example, has over 17,000,000 inhabitants, compared with 11,500,000 in the capital city, Beijing. *Mumbai* (Bombay) in India has 18,000,000 inhabitants, compared to the 10,000,000 in *New Delhi*. The population of *New York* is 17,000,000, whereas that of *Washington*, the capital city, is only 4,000,000.

FACT

Tokyo, with 26,400,000 inhabitants is the most heavily populated city in the world. Second is Mexico City with 18,200,000 inhabitants, followed by Sao Paolo in Brazil, with 17,800,000 inhabitants.

View of Singapore

Traffic in Hong Kong

View of Shanghai, China

SUCH TRAFFIC!

Suva *on the island of Fiji is the city with the most cars on the road - 668 for each 1000 inhabitants. People in* **Kathmandu** *in Nepal,* **Mbale** *in Uganda and* **Tangail** *in Bangladesh are unlikely to suffocate from traffic fumes - there are only three vehicles for each 1000 residents. At* **Tbilisi**, *in Georgia and* **Yerevan** *in Armenia 98% of the inhabitants use public transport. In remote places such as* **Porto Novo** *in the West African country of Benin, there is no traffic at all...*

Languages

Chinese Mandarin is the language spoken most in the world - 1,075,000,000 people use it for conversation, to conduct business and in everyday speech. **English** is the second most spoken language, used by over half a billion people, and the 'official language' of at least 54 countries. Third place is occupied equally between **Spanish**, the 'official language' of 21 countries and Hindi which is spoken by about 425,000,000 people. Next comes **Russian**, then **Arabic**, adopted language in 24 countries, followed by **Portuguese**, the 'official language' of eight countries and used by almost 200,000,000 individuals. Although **French** is the 'official language' in 33 countries, fewer people speak this language than speak **Bengali** - 130,000,000 speaking French, 215,000,000 speaking Bengali.

Outside Italy, Italian is spoken in the Canton Ticino in Switzerland and in the Republic of San Marino - around 62,000,000 million people in total. Between them, the people of the world speak and write in over 6000 languages. But over one third of the world population use the six which are most widespread. Some experts believe that there are 426 languages close to extinction.

Chinese and Tibetan children gathered together around an accordionist in Turkmenistan, S.W.Asia

A man from Turkmenistan

Far from home

About 2-3% of the world population, that is about 120 - 180 million people, live outside their place of birth. These are people who have emigrated. Emigration arises from various social and economic factors - the unemployed go to find work, there are wars and political persecution, famine and epidemics.
The highest number of immigrants (people living outside their native land) live in Asia - 43 million. 25 million immigrants live in **Europe**, 24 million immigrants live in the **United States** and **Canada**, and 15.5 million refugees are spread throughout various **African countries**. An estimated 7.5 million immigrants live in **Latin America**. The highest number of immigrants in relation to the native population live in **Oceania**, the continent which includes Australia. Here, almost five million out of a total of 31.5 million people are immigrants.

The need for food

On average, every person, each day in the major industrialized countries consumes 3500 calories of food. In many other countries, this is reduced to 2000 and 3000 calories. Half the world's population regularly consumes far less than 2000 calories each day, suffering famine and malnutrition.

HOW THE WORLD EATS

Every person in an average **United States** *city consumes at least 146 grams of fats and 114 grams of protein per day - three times the amount consumed by the average African. The average food intake of a South American is the diet highest in nutrition comprising 156 grams of fats and 166 protein.*
During the last 40 years the only continent to have improved its diet significantly is Asia - but this is where the staple diet is based on cereals. Africa still remains the continent where famine and malnutrition claims the most victims, especially among children. In the poorest areas, people either have nothing to eat at all, or have to eat plant (not vegetable) products with a low calorie content.

A group of immigrants

Religions

The four most widespread religions in the world are - **Christianity**, with 2 billion followers, then **Islam**, with 1.2 billion, **Hindu**, with 900 million and **Buddhism**, with 400 million. Next comes the **Sikh** religion with 23 million followers, and the **Hebrew** or **Jewish** faith with 15 million. One sixth of the world population are said to be atheist or agnostic and do not follow any religious faith. Indonesia has a higher number of Muslims than in any other country - 165,000,000. In India, the Hindus number more than 850,000,000, the largest number of followers of this faith. A quarter of all Buddhists, around 100,000,000, live in Japan and many more in China, whilst the majority of believers who belong to the Christian and Jewish faiths live in the United States - 230,000,000 Christian and 6,000,000 Jewish - more followers of the Jewish faith than those living in Israel.

Buddhist monks in Bangkok, Thailand.

Muslims at prayer in Calcutta, India.

Ritual Hindu bathing at Varanasi, Benares, India.

Good Friday procession on the island of
Procida in the Bay of Naples

135

The world leader in commerce is not the United States, as one might expect, but the European Union to which 15 European states belong. The European Union controls 16.6% of the total world exports, compared to 15.2% by the United States. But the United States lead Europe in terms of goods and services - 15.9% in goods, compared to 15.2% by Europe, and 20% in services compared to around 18%.

Bosses of power

Bill Gates, President of Microsoft, world leader in the computer sector, is top of the list of multi-millionaire magnates, with wealth estimated at least 90 billion American dollars. Two of his fellow countrymen follow close behind - Larry Ellison, with an estimated wealth of 47 billion dollars and Warren Edward Buffet, with a personal fortune estimated at 36 billion dollars. The Sultan of Brunei and the King of Saudi Arabia each have a more modest amount of 30 billion American dollars. The French woman Lilliane Bettencourt, heiress of the Oréal cosmetics empire, is the woman thought to be the richest in the world, with a personal fortune estimated at least 14.9 billion dollars.

The Chrysler building in New York

LAND OF THE WEALTHY

It is believed that there are at least 73 multi-millionaires living in the United States, each with a personal fortune of not less than one billion American dollars. The list includes 18 German multi-millionaires, 12 Japanese, eight Chinese, seven each French, Mexican and Saudi and six Italian.
The money at their disposal would be enough to settle the foreign debts of many poor countries. There are more multi-millionaires in the world today than there have ever been before.

137

Cereals, vegetables, fruit and grain

China holds the world record for the production of cereals (455 billion tonnes), meat (61.5 billion tonnes), fruit (67.8 billion tonnes) and vegetables (260 billion tonnes) - compared to the ***United States***, which produces 335.5 billion tonnes of cereals and 37.2 billion tonnes of meats and ***India*** for plant foodstuffs (38.5 billion tonnes of fruit and 59.4 billion tonnes of vegetables). One sixth of the agricultural production is grown in ***China***, which is also at the top of the table, in both the production and the consumption of rice and grain - 198.4 billion tonnes of rice produced, which is one third of the world total, and 114 billion tonnes consumed. ***Brazil*** takes top place in the cultivation and production of sugar and coffee - 20,600 tonnes of sugar and 1941 million tonnes of coffee. ***India*** and ***China*** on their own, with 806,000 and 676,000 tonnes, harvest more tea than all the other countries in the world put together. The ***Ivory Coast*** is the world leader in the production of cocoa - 1,163,000 tonnes per year. Half of this, 656,000 tonnes, is exported to the United States.

Pure natural wool

Australia produces the most natural wool - 673,000 tonnes. Unexpectedly, after *China*, the top consumer of wool is *Italy*. *China* is the foremost producer of cotton worldwide - 3,829,000 tonnes compared to 3,694,000 tonnes in the *United States* and 2,562,000 tonnes in *India*.

WATER AND LIFE

Drinking water is a precious resource in all countries. As populations, industry and agriculture increase, so water becomes all the more valuable. However, in many countries, there are not enough sources of clear, pure water. Often, there is no water at all.

In **North** *and* **Central America**, *each person drinks on average 280,900 litres of water each year. In* **Oceania**, *the amount is 147,1000 litres, in* **Europe** *139,500 litres, and in* **Asia**, *103,800. In* **South America** *the figure drops to 74,700 litres per person, whilst in* **Africa** *it plunges to 45,900 litres.*

Harvesting barley in China

FACT

The **United States** is the major producer as well as the major consumer of natural and synthetic rubber - 2,350,000 tonnes per year. **Thailand** is the second largest, producing 2,240,000 tonnes per year.

A little energy for many people

In the **United States** and **Canada**, the average person uses approximately twice the amount of energy as a **European**, ten times more than an **Asian** and 20 times more than an **African**. The **United States** alone uses over one quarter of the petroleum produced in the world. According to recent estimates, in the course of an average lifetime, each American uses 28 tonnes of animal products, such as meat, dairy goods and animal fats, 25 tonnes of vegetable product, 770 tonnes of mineral origin and a quantity of energy equivalent to 4000 barrels of petrol.

In **Asia** there has been a progressive, almost explosive increase in economic growth, accompanied by an increase in the number of consumers. For example - in less than 50 years, the Chinese economy has increased more than ten times, and the number of consumers has grown by 18 times. In less than twenty years, **China** has also doubled its use of coal, and this releases into the atmosphere vast quantities of harmful carbon dioxide - even more than in the United States - with serious consequences for the environment.

The consumption of energy per person in the developing **Asiatic countries** such as India and Taiwan is still much lower than that of larger industrialized nations, although the gap does narrow from year to year.

In eastern **European** countries such as the Czech Republic, Latvia and Estonia, the fall of the Communist regimes has been followed by problems resulting in the diminishing of energy supply and consumption.

Nuclear power station in France

Hydroelectric station in Siberia, Russia

Windmills in the Mancia region, Spain

Oil wells in Libya

This has led to a reduction in the amounts of carbon dioxide released into the air, and a complete re-organization of the economy. The result has been the ending of many out-of-date working practices and a more efficient use of energy resources.

Of all regions in the world, *Africa* is the continent which has seen the largest growth in population. It is also the continent suffering the most from drought and consequent poverty. Famine is a serious problem, and this is often caused by continual civil wars and political unrest, combined with a lack of any proper foundation for proper government in many African countries. There are eighteen countries in the world with insufficient water resources. Six of these are in *Africa*, and another six African countries are close to

being added to this list.

One quarter of renewable water resources, such as hydro-electricity, are in *Latin America*. But, although hydroelectric energy is a very important resource for the people of Latin America, (over 60% of energy used comes from the great hydroelectric stations) the emissions of carbon dioxide, not to mention the devastation caused by fires breaking out in the Amazon rain forest, result in more damage to the environment than in other continents.

In *Oceania* the percentage of agricultural and fertile land is still very high. The population of this whole continent is the same as Tokyo, but distributed across an area which is more extensive than that of the United States, and which enables a massive cultivation of cereals, fruit and vegetables.

Coal mine in Britain

Geo-thermic Centre in Iceland

Wind farm on the island of Lanzarote, Spain

Oil-rig platform in the North Sea

Energy and resources

Saudi Arabia extracts from its oil wells at least 8,595,000 barrels of petroleum each day. Only a fraction of this is used by the country itself. The **United States** consumes an estimated 7,760,000 barrels per day and **Russia**, 6,180,000 barrels. The highest consumption of crude oil is in the most advanced industrial countries - the **United States**, using 18,490,000 barrels per day, **Japan** using 5,650,000, **China** using 4,370,000 and **Germany** using 2,825,000 barrels. **Russia** and the **United States** lead the way both in the production and the consumption of natural gas - 551 billion cubic metres extracted by the **United States** and 540 billion cubic metres used, compared to 364 billion cubic metres extracted by **Russia** and 617 billion cubic metres used. The **United States** and **China** are also the major producers as well as consumers, of coal. The **United States** mines 580 million TEP (Tonnes of Equivalent energy to Petroleum) and 512 million TEP is mined by **Russia**. In each case, the coal produced is necessary for the country's own needs.

Oil wells in Saudi Arabia

Diamond mine at Kimberley, South Africa

THE MAJOR PRODUCERS

The **United States** *are world leaders in the production of energy resources, producing each year 2.5 billion tonnes of coal equivalent, followed by* **Russia***, with 1.4 billion tonnes,* **China***, 1.3 billion tonnes and* **Saudi Arabia***, with 665 million tonnes. Coal equivalent is a way of comparing how much energy countries make and use from fossil fuels, renewable and nuclear energy sources. Among the major consumers we find, as always, the countries with the strongest economies.* **China** *is becoming increasingly important as a consumer, often preceded in statistical tables only by the* **United States***. For example, China's annual consumption is 1.2 billion tonnes of coal equivalent, compared to 3.1 billion tonnes by the United States.*

Sources of energy

The source of energy most widely used is *petroleum* (3.2 billion tonnes per year - 40% of the total energy used), followed by *coal* (2.2 billion tonnes of petrol equivalent - 27% of total energy used), then *methane gas* (1.9 billion tonnes of TEP - 23% of total energy used) and nuclear energy (596 million tonnes of TEP - 7% of the total energy used). *Hydro-electric* energy and *alternative energy* constitute barely 3% of total energy resources. As far as nuclear power stations are concerned, there are 110 working nuclear reactors in the United States, 57 in France, and 53 in Japan.

Oil extraction plant in Cuba

Technician working in a Nuclear Power Station in Britain

Gold and diamonds

South Africa is world leader in the mining and production of *diamonds* - 40 million carats per year, compared to 17 million carats from the *Democratic Republic of the Congo*, and approximately the same total from *Russia*.

South Africa leads the world in the mining and production of *gold*, with 447.2 tonnes mined each year. The *United States* comes next with 341 tonnes, followed by *Australia* with 300 tonnes. Approximately half the world's gold reserves (77,000 tonnes) are in South Africa, also half the world's reserves of *platinum*. First in the production of silver is *Mexico* with 2467 tonnes per year, followed by *Peru*, with 2217 tonnes, and the *United States* with 1952 tonnes. *Canada* is the undisputed leader in the production of *uranium* - 10,515 tonnes per year, as compared to the next largest producer, *Australia*, with 3712 tonnes.

FACT

Japan is world leader in the production of motor cars, manufacturing an estimated eight million vehicles per year. Second is the *United States*, with 6.5 million cars and then *Germany* with over 4 million cars.

Diamond mine in Brazil

The Central German Bank, Frankfurt

144

Banking, commerce and investment

In the field of **banking**, among the ten most important for funds and finances, three are **American** (two of which are at the top of the classification) and four **Japanese**. At tenth place is a **Chinese** Bank, *the Industrial and Commercial Bank of China*. At the highest place is the United States *Citigroup* with funds of 47,699 million American dollars. Among the **giant business enterprises** worldwide, first place goes to Microsoft, the company owned by Bill Gates, with a capital of 586 billion American dollars. Close behind, with 474 billion American dollars, another **United States** Company, *General Electric*. At third place, the Japanese-owned *NTT Mobile*, with a capital of 366 billion dollars, followed by companies leading the field in international telecommunications.

Leading manufacturers

Among the ten largest *manufacturers* in the world, six are US-owned and four Japanese. At the top is *General Motors* with a turnover of 176.6 million American dollars, followed by the *Ford Motor Company* and *Daimler-Chrysler* in the car sector.

The Tokyo Stock Exchange

School and study

Gabon is the country with the highest number of pupils at elementary school. But only 67% of these are of school age - which shows that it is not only children who seek basic education, but also people who for some reason have had to discontinue school, without having finished schooling, or those who have not yet reached a good level of study because of social problems or personal reasons. The West African states of **Niger** and **Burkina Faso** have the least number of pupils in basic education, 29% of the total number of school-aged children in Niger and 40% in Burkina Faso, a sign that only a minority of children reach the first stage of education. Not surprisingly, only 14.3% of the total population of Niger and 20.7% of Burkina Faso's population can read and write. These countries have the lowest levels of literacy in the world.

Canada is the nation with the most students at University.

Elementary school in the Cameroon

The percentage of University students in **Italy** is 47%, which is lower than **Germany** and **Holland**, but higher than **Israel** (44%) and **Japan** (43%).

Moldavia is the country which invests most in its educational system - 10.6% of its GNP (Gross National Product or total revenue) followed by **Namibia** and **Zimbabwe**, with a percentage of approximately 9%, which is higher than countries in Northern Europe. **Jamaica**, **Yemen**, **Jordan**, **Cuba** and **Kenya** also spend a lot on education, between 6.5% and 7.5% of GNP. **China**, a country which in the past few years has undergone massive economic development, spends only 2.5% GNP on the education of their young people. **Nigeria**, spending 0.7% GNP and the **Sudan**, spending 0.9% GNP are last on the list - but it has to be remembered that both countries are afflicted with problems such as war, political revolutions, economic crises, famine and under-development.

Let's talk

The **United States** takes the lead in the field of computers. Approximately 51% of all Americans own a personal computer (about 141 million people) compared to 38% **British** and 30% **Japanese**.
Users of the Internet worldwide are estimated at 300 million, 38% of whom are **American** or **Canadian** (an estimated 140 million), 30% European (Scandinavia are at the head of this classification with 70 million users) and 9% Japanese. All other users of the network make up the remaining 23%.
In the whole of the **Middle East** and **Africa**, the number of people using the World-Wide Web is no more than 4 million.

Public telephones in Johannesburg, South Africa

Who's there?

In **Bermuda** there are 85.7 telephone lines for every 100 people, which is more than in **Norway** (about 73). In the **United States** the number is 67.3 telephone lines for each 100 people.

However, there are many places in the world where the telephone has not yet arrived. It is largely an unobtainable luxury in the **Democratic Republic of the Congo**, also in large parts of **Africa** (in **Tanzania** there is one telephone for each 200 people); in **Cambodia**, in **Bangladesh** and in **Laos**. But also in European countries such as **Romania**, the **Ukraine** and **Poland**, there are no more than 16 telephone lines for each 100 people. In **Albania** the number is estimated at three! Very low on the list of telephone-users is **South America** where only **Chile** and **Argentina**

barely reach 20 telephones for each 100 people.

Luxembourg has the highest percentage of owners of cellular (mobile) telephones in the world - 87.2 telephones per 100 people. **Austria** and **Italy** occupy the second and third places respectively - 78.6 telephones per 100 people in Austria, 73.7 telephones per 100 inhabitants in Italy. The number of users of mobile telephones in **Scandinavian** countries is higher than **Germany**, **France**, **Japan**, and even the **United States**, where there are only 31.6 mobile telephones in use for each 100 people. The average figure worldwide is 5.5% instruments for each 100 people. But in **Africa** mobile telephones are widely unknown, as they are in countries such as **Vietnam**, **Nepal** and parts of **Pakistan**.

A typical red telephone box in the UK

FACT

The United States have the highest number of telephone kiosks spread across their vast country (approximately 1,800,000), whilst in Japan there are 830,000 telephone kiosks.

Books, CDs, magazines, videos

Canada is a real paradise for the 'home video'! Here, there are 89.9 video recorders per 100 families.

The *United States* is world leader in the sale of books - 27 million are sold each year, compared with ten million sold in Japan and in Germany, partly due to the complex population of these two countries.

In *Norway*, each person spends the equivalent to 127 American dollars on magazines.

In *Hong Kong*, 762 magazines are sold for each 1000 people, in *Macao* 533, and in the *United States* 203. Bottom of this table are *Panama*, *Lebanon* and *Uruguay*.

Book market at Tunis

FACT

The best-selling book of all time is The Bible, closely followed by the Works of William Shakespeare. The only book to have outsold The Bible in the USA in one month was *Gone With The Wind* by Margaret Mitchell. The *most prolific children's author* is Enid Blyton, with over 450 books published, as well as short stories, poems, plays and articles.

The **United States** and **Japan** are also at the head of the 'hit parade' of discs, audio-cassettes and CDs sold - over 14 million in the United States, 6.5 million in Japan. **Brazil**, **Mexico** and **Spain** are low on the list, each country buying a combined total of only 500,000.

People in **Iceland** spend less than any other country - just 55 American dollars per head.

Book-stall in Havana, Cuba

Book sale at Berlin
University, Germany

The production of waste

A rubbish dump in
Rio de Janeiro, Brazil

The traditional villages and nomad camps throughout Africa, Asia and Latin America produce a modest amount of waste, because they only produce and consume what they need. In contrast, the richest countries in the world produce vast quantities of domestic and industrial waste. It is calculated that in the *United States*, each citizen produces on average 730 kilograms of rubbish per year, compared to 690 in *Australia* and 660 in *Canada*. Of all the ten nations at the top of this table, none produce less than half a tonne of rubbish per year per person.

Fresh Kills on Staten Island, New York in the United States is the largest rubbish processing plant in the world. It extends over a surface of 1200 hectares (equal to 2400 American football stadiums) the central body is as tall as a 17-storey building and it can contain up to 100 million tonnes of rubbish, the processing of which produces an estimated 2700 tonnes of methane gas.

Deforestation and the guardianship of the environment

Each year, more than 70,000 sq. km. of tropical rain forest is being destroyed by the harvesting of wood or cultivating land. **Brazil** is the country where most trees are chopped down - the average annual table is 22,264 sq. km. of forest, compared with 13,124 sq. km. in **Indonesia** and 9549 sq. km. in the **Sudan**. The most rapid deforestation is in **Burundi**, where each year 9% of the forest area vanishes. In **Indonesia**, the percentage is about 1.2%. In **Gabon**, 84% of the territory is still covered by forest, 82% in **Guinea Bissau** (formerly Portuguese Guinea), West Africa. Both these countries have even more trees than 'the land of forests' **Finland**, which has 72% of forest area.

Finland, **Norway**, **Canada**, **Sweden** and **Switzerland** are the countries which show most respect for their natural surroundings. This is shown in the ESI (Environmental Sustainability Index) classification which measures the level of progress towards environmental sustainability between different countries, with a value of 80 out of 100 maximum. Most other nations are a little below this. Last on the list as far as ecological awareness is concerned are **North Korea** with a value of 32 out of 100, the **United Arab Emirates** (26/100) and **Kuwait** (24/100).

Deforestation in Benin

Earthquakes

Earthquakes happen when the tectonic plates which form the outer crust of the Earth move or push violently against each other. This collision causes powerful **seismic waves**. When these seismic waves reach the surface, they make the Earth tremble and shake with their force. This is an earthquake.

Earthquakes happen most of all in zones where the Earth's crust is most likely to move, such as along the edge of the tectonic plates. They usually cause untold damage and claim the lives of many victims. The most devastating earthquake of all times was probably on the 2 February 1556, in the province of **Shanshi** in China, when at least 820,000 people lost their lives in just a few instants. Other 'historic' earthquakes were recorded 20 May 526 in **Antioch**, Syria claiming 250,000 victims, and on 11 October 1737 in **Calcutta**, India, with victims estimated at 3000. In recent years, on 28 July 1976, in the province of Tangshan one quarter of the population was killed and an untold number of homes destroyed by an earthquake.

A team of rescue-workers at work after the earthquake at Messina in 1908

Explosions and fires caused by the breakage of tubes of gas, accompany only the most violent of earthquakes

FACT

Each year throughout the world about 800 earthquakes of intense force are recorded, whilst each day we can count at least 8000 minor tremors which, in general, do not cause any damage. The longest earthquake ever recorded, four minutes, was in **Alaska** in 1964.

The earthquake at **Kobe** in Japan, in January 1995, holds the record for the most costly natural disaster, with damage amounting to more than 100 billion dollars. **China**, **Japan**, **Iran**, **India**, **Turkey**, have each lost an enormous number of their people due to the movement of the Earth's crust, and also in **Italy** there have been serious earthquakes in **Belice**, **Friuli** in **Irpina** and more recently in **Umbria** and **Marche**. The earthquake at Messina on 28 December 1908 was most disastrous of all, causing the deaths of 160,000 people.

Two pictures of the devastation caused by the earthquake which destroyed the countries of Irpina, in the region of Campania, in 1980

Volcanic eruptions

Most volcanoes are found along the cracks in the Earth's crust. The flowing mantle of the Earth pushes up towards the surface, searching for ways to escape. If the crust is too dense, the mantle flows back. In time it escapes, exploding like a cork from a bottle, and a volcano is 'born'.

Some volcanic eruptions are more easily remembered than others - for example, the eruption which in the second millennium BC devastated the island of **Santorini** and destroyed the Minoan civilization. Even more famous was the eruption on 24 August 79 AD, when the Roman cities of **Pompeii** and **Herculeum** were buried under a thick layer of lava, cinders and ash from the volcano **Vesuvius**.

The explosion of the volcano **Krakatoa**, on the island of Omonima, in the Indonesian islands, on 26-27 August 1883, was heard over 4000 kilometres distance and was, without doubt, the greatest volcanic eruption ever recorded. The most horrific was that of the volcano **Tambora** (see picture) on **Sumbawa**, also in Indonesia, the most volcanic country on Earth. Between 5 and 12 April 1815 the eruption claimed 92,000 victims. It also changed the climate of the region for many years, and the colour of the sky at sunset shone in an unreal way.

A flood of lava descends from the mouth of Etna

The eruption of Mont Saint Helens with over 57 victims caused the collapse of the summit and an entire side of the volcano

RECENT VOLCANIC ERUPTIONS

In the course of the last century, two volcanic eruptions were particularly violent. First, was the eruption of **Mount Pelée** *on the Caribbean island of Martinique, which on 8 May 1902, seemed to swallow up entire villages, the capital of Saint-Pierre and over 34,000 inhabitants in a cloud of shining gas. Second was the eruption of the Columbian volcano* **Nevado del Ruiz** *on 13 November 1985. This was so fierce that it caused the sudden melting of an expanse of ice, resulting in a flooding of water and mud called Lahar, which descended on 25,000 helpless victims at its foot.*

FACT

Etna is one of the most famous volcanoes in the world. On 11 March 1660 an eruption completely destroyed the city of Catania.

Fires

Fire has destroyed cities, countries, places of culture, famous monuments, works of art, public places and places of natural beauty. One of the most famous is when the Roman Emperor *Nero*, in 64 AD is said to have played his violin as *Rome* burned. According to legend, he remained quite unconcerned about its total destruction. At the time Rome had over one million inhabitants and the wall around the city was 20 kilometres long. *The Great Fire of London* in 1666 was another famous fire, when sparks from a baker's oven in Pudding Lane gradually spread to engulf most of the wooden buildings of the old city in flames. This fire led to the formation of a proper fire brigade and also companies to insure people against loss by fire.

FIRE AND FLAMES

The most destructive fires of the 19th century were those which took place in the last years of that century.
In 1983 a large part of southern **Australia** *was devastated by fire. In 1988, a series of fires, caused by dry air and lightning reduced to cinders 320,000 hectares of forest in the* **Yellowstone National Park***, in the United States.*
In the summer of 1998 the skies over the whole of **Indonesia** *were blotted out by an enormous cloud of smoke which remained suspended in the air for months, as the result of numerous blazes in the forests of* **Sumatra** *and* **Kalimantan** *in* **Borneo** *(see picture). The area affected was more vast than the whole of Europe, with serious consequences for the health of the people in many Indonesian countries. In the fog caused by the flames, the visibility was so poor that some ships ran aground and others collided. An aeroplane crashed on the island of Sumatra killing 200 people.*

Different classes of fire

Forest fires apply to trees and plants which are more than 1.8m in height. A forest fire spreads most rapidly through the top branches of trees, before burning the lower branches and the undergrowth. Most often forest fires break out after a long, hot spell of weather, sometimes from something as small as a discarded matchstick or a glass bottle which has attracted heat from the Sun.
Wildland or *brush fires* is the classification for trees and plants less than 1.8m tall. Very often the heat from a forest fire will make evergreen and conifer trees burst into flames.

The fire which destroyed part of the Australian forest in 1983, photographed from a satellite

RECORD NEWS
THE
WORLD
AROUND US

The world around us is constantly changing. Sometimes these changes happen naturally. Over the years, a river may change its course when its banks are widened by rain and flood-water. The shape of a coastline may change through erosion of the ground, landslides or collapses of land. The eruption of volcanoes can flatten the landscape and changes in the climate can transform fertile land into areas of desert, or melt glaciers of ice, so that sea levels rise and flood surrounding areas.

Sometimes, changes to our world are made by us, the people living on the planet. As a result of war or civil dispute, land is often gained or lost, and this changes the boundaries of a country, often its name and its economy - which means, how wealthy the country is.

As industry increased worldwide, roads, railways, canals and large harbours were built, criss-crossing vast expanses of land and by-passing mountains. Small villages became small towns and small towns became cities. Now, motorways have altered the shape of many of our towns and the extent of our open spaces. More industry and increasing development has led to a better standard of living for people in many countries. It has also contributed to many problems which we now see increasing. For instance, the use of chlorofluorocarbons (CFC gases) in aerosol sprays, packaging and refrigeration systems has made a 'hole' in the ozone layer over the Antarctic. The ozone layer shields the Earth from harmful ultraviolet radiation from the sun, so any weakening in this layer will have serious consequences, unless action is taken to prevent it going any further.

The burning of fossil fuels and deforestation of rain forests have created what is known as the 'greenhouse effect', where carbon dioxide released into the air and water vapour in the atmosphere prevents heat escaping from the Earth. This causes 'global warming' - a general rise in the temperature of the climate. Already we are seeing ice-caps at the Antarctic beginning to melt, leading to a rise in the levels of the surrounding seas, with the threat of serious flooding and land erosion.

'Acid rain' is a term used to describe rainfall which is polluted by carbon dioxide and other gases released into the air by the burning of fossil fuels, also the exhaust fumes from road and railway vehicles. Acid rain can destroy vast areas of pasture, open spaces and places of natural beauty.

Who knows what our world will be like in another fifty years? There are certain to be even more changes.

WORLD RECORDS
TRANSPORT

Roads and cars

The total length of all roads in the **United States** is the longest in the world - 6,438,227 kilometres (km.). **India** has the second longest - 3,319,644 km., then **Brazil** with 1,724,924 km. **China**, a vast country, has only 1,210,000 km. of roads. Yet **Japan**, which is 26 times smaller than **China**, has 1,152,207 km. It is estimated that in the **United States** there are 150 million vehicles in circulation - that is 30% of the total number of vehicles in the world. Compare this number to the 40 million cars in **Japan** and in **Germany**, and more than 30 million in **Italy**. In **Russia**, the largest country in the world, the number is about 15.5 million.

Macau, on the coast of the South China Sea, has a higher density of roads than any other country - at least 15.2 km. of road for each sq.km.

The need for roads must also take into account the size of the country. For instance, the small island of **Malta** has 5.51 km. of road for each sq. km.; the island of **Singapore**, 4.80 km., and the small country of **Belgium** 4.78 km. The **United States** is a huge country, so there are no restrictions on space to build roads.

Hong Kong has the most crowded roads, with 287 vehicles per kilometre. This means that 700 metres for each 1000 metres of road is occupied by some method of transport. Close behind Hong Kong is the **Arab United Emirates**, with 232 vehicles for each kilometre and **Macau**, with 199 vehicles per kilometre.

KEEP MOVING!

The **Lebanon** is the country with the highest amount of road traffic with 732 cars for each 1000 inhabitants. This is even higher than the traffic in wealthier and more developed countries such as **Luxembourg** (576), **Brunei** (576), and **Italy** (545). The **United States** has 'only' 486 cars per 1000 inhabitants.

Somalia in Africa and **Tajikistan** in Central Asia are the countries with the lowest amount of road traffic, each with 0.1 vehicle for each thousand inhabitants. This means that in **Somalia** there are no more than one thousand cars.

Left hand page - New York traffic. Centre spread - the stream of traffic on the 'Golden Gate' bridge, San Francisco. Above, taxi and car chaos in Calcutta, India.

FACT

Horse power is part of the specification of any engine-powered vehicle. This dates from the time when all traffic was horse-drawn. The strength or pulling power of an engine was measured against the strength of the horse and expressed as horse power. A 12-horse power engine pulls at twelve times the power of a horse.

Roads, intersections, bridges and junctions

The longest road in the world is the **Pan-American Highway**. This is a network of highways which connect North America to South America and includes the Inter-American Highway, which goes from Nuevo Laredo in Mexico to Panama City, a distance of 5,390 km. The length of the entire Pan-American Highway is over 9000 kilometres. The widest road is the **Monumental Axis**, an enormous highway of three lanes, each more than 250 metres wide and 2.5 km. long, which connects the Plaza Municipal with the 'Tre Poteri' Plaza of the Three Towers in Brasilia, bustling capital city of Brazil. The narrowest main road is known as '**The Alley of Manliness**' in Ripatransone, in the Italian province of Ascoli Picena, in which the widest part does not exceed 43 centimetres.

The motorway with the most lanes - 23 - is the **Bridge Toll Plaza** which connects San Francisco (USA) with Oakland Bay, crossing the famous Golden Gate bridge. The steepest main road is **Baldwin Street** in Dunedin, New Zealand, with a gradient of 42.2% - hence the danger signals advising motorcyclists to dismount. Just compare this gradient to the steepest road in San Francisco, an African footpath or a mountain pass with a gradient of 31%!

Road through the Andes mountains in Peru.

MOTOR CAR MANUFACTURERS

The American company **General Motors** *is the largest manufacturer of cars. Each day over 7 million vehicles leave its production lines for private and commercial use. Second largest is another old-established American manufacturer, the* **Ford Motor Company**, *with over 5 million cars, followed by the Japanese* **Toyota**, *with about 5 million cars.*

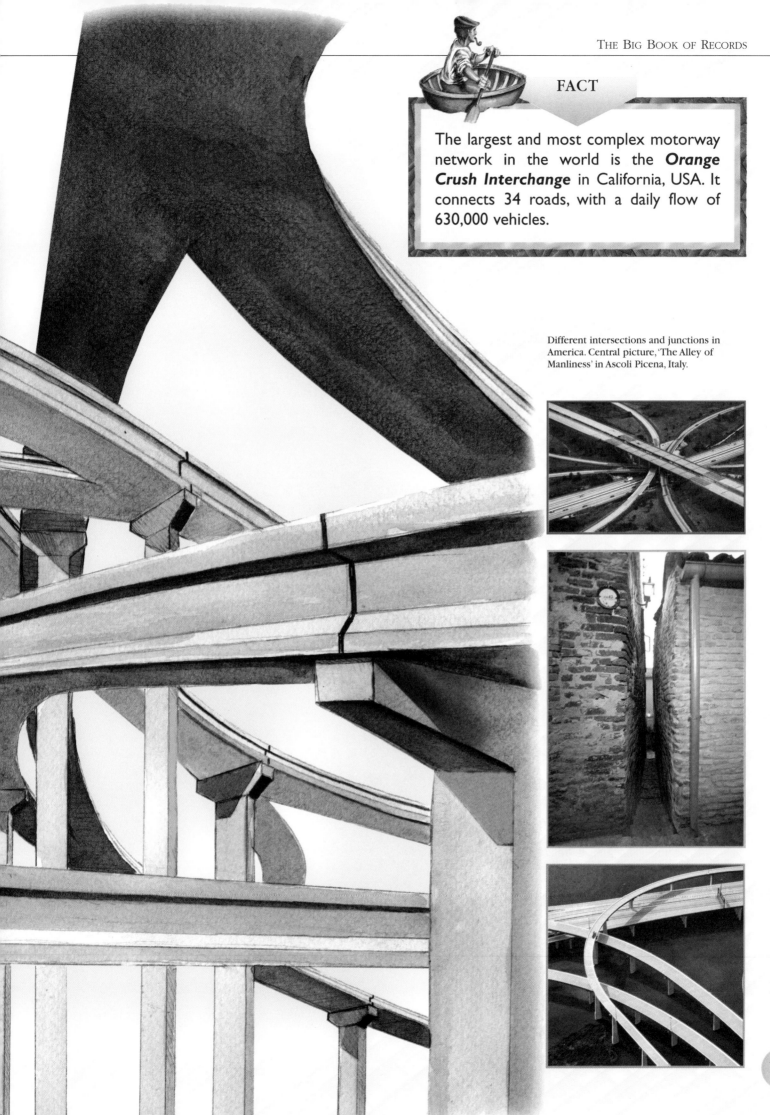

The largest and most complex motorway network in the world is the **Orange Crush Interchange** in California, USA. It connects 34 roads, with a daily flow of 630,000 vehicles.

Different intersections and junctions in America. Central picture, 'The Alley of Manliness' in Ascoli Picena, Italy.

Like a torpedo...

The **Lamborghini Diablo 5.7** at its maximum of 492-horse power can reach the speed of 325 km. per hour, 5 km. faster than the **Ferrari 550 M**. The most expensive is the **Bugatti Royal Sports Coupé** model 41 of 1931. Only six of these cars were ever made. They all passed from private ownership to a Japanese society in 1990, for a price of 15 million American dollars. The Formula 1 racing car goes like a rocket! The teams **Ferrari**, **Williams** and **McLaren** are always competing for world championships, the title of the fastest performance car, and to beat the fastest lap circuit record, nearly 350 kilometres per hour!

A revolutionary world land speed record was established by Scots-born Andrew Green in October 1997 in the Nevada Desert, driving **Thrust SSC**, a British-built car weighing 6.4 tonnes. This car broke through the sound barrier (centre picture) and was able to reach 1228 kilometres an hour because it was powered by a 110,000-horse power jet reactor consuming about 20 litres of fuel per second instead of an engine.

The largest vehicle in the world is a German-made RB 293 **Bucket Wheel Excavator** weighing 14,196 tonnes and used in a coal mine in Westphalia. It is 220 metres long, 95 metres in height and can excavate and deposit up to 240,000 cubic metres of soil per day.

FACT

The German **Volkswagen 'Beetle'** is the most popular car of all time. Production ceased in 1978, after almost 50 years. During that time, over 20 million Volkswagen 'Beetles' had been produced and sold.

A famous Bugatti car

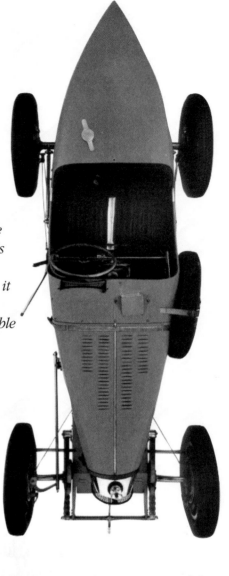

A SWIMMING POOL IN A CAR

The longest car, cumbersome, but also the most unusual in the world, is the **Limousine**, *the project of Jay Ohrberg from Burbank, California, USA. This car is more than 30 metres long and goes along on 26 wheels. It can be driven like 'straight out', but it is articulated (jointed) at the centre, so that it can handle curves or U-turns. Among the car's 'extras' there is a bar, a dressing room, even a swimming pool with a diving board and a comfortable bed with a water mattress! The* **Limousine** *will probably be used mostly on film sets and as a venue for important people to meet on special occasions.*

THRUST 2-trust securities

On four wheels...

The largest **service station** in the world is in Saudi Arabia. Here, a motorist can 'fill up' at any one of the 200 fuel pumps which occupy an area larger than one quarter of a sizeable city.

The biggest trucks in the world are those which pull **road-trains**. Huge trailers are linked together to make the train which is pulled by the truck, rather like a locomotive pulling wagons. Road-trains travel through areas where there are no railways, such as the central zones of Australia. Here, road-trains go along the Great Eastern Highway through Western Australia. The longest-ever road 'convoy' was recorded at Merredin, Western Australia on 19 October 2000. One lorry pulled 79 trailers which stretched for over 1018 metres.

The fastest **fire engine** in the world is the Hawaiian Eagle, which on 11 July 1998, at Brainerd in Florida, USA, reached a speed of 355 km. per hour. The fire engine Oshkosh of Wisconsin is slower on the road, but it can eject 190,000 litres of extinguisher foam in less than 3 minutes - a real life-saving record!

At the bottom of the sea

The **bathyscaphe Trieste** (see centre picture) was built in Switzerland for the United States Navy. On 23 January 1960, with Jacques Piccard and Donald Welsh on board, the Trieste descended 10,911 metres to the greatest ocean depth in the world, the Marianna Trench in the Pacific Ocean.

FACT

The largest **tyres** are those mounted on lorries built to transport heavy building materials and exceptional loads. These tyres can have a diameter of 3.6 metres, which is twice the height of a man.

The first **nameplates** on cars had appeared by the end of the 1800s.

The American manufacturer Oldsmobile was the first to produce particular models of cars in any numbers.

The mechanical **windscreen wiper** came into use in 1910. Electrically-powered lights were first mounted in cars in 1912.

Left-hand page, an American fire engine: above, the gigantic trailer trucks of Canada.

Escalators

The longest **escalator** in the world is the Central Mid-Levels Escalator Link in Hong Kong, a complex system of escalators and walkways more than 800 metres long, used for the transport of goods and people at the Central Market of the city. The 'shortest' are those used in the Okadaya More Shopping Mall, Kawasaki-shi, Japan, only 83 centimetres high, 20 times smaller than a normal escalator.

Aircraft and airports

America is the world leader regarding the use of aircraft. On average, each American citizen flies ten times more than a **Japanese**, or a person from the UK. Not surprisingly, the most frequently used airports in the world are **Hartsfield** in **Atlanta**, with 80 million passengers, the **O'Hare** airport in **Chicago** with 72 million passengers and the **Los Angeles International Airport** with 68.5 million each year. Over 2500 flights leave each airport every day.

London's Heathrow is the airport where most passengers embark on inter-continental flights - 62 million each year. In the United States there are 14,574 airports - many more than other countries which can boast a high number of airports. For example, **Brazil** has 3291 airports, **Russia** 2517. The heaviest cargo transported by air was a Space Shuttle almost 40 metres long and weighing over 100 tonnes. A **Boeing 747** (see picture) which had to be especially modified transported the Space Shuttle from the space station at Cape Canaveral to the launch site.

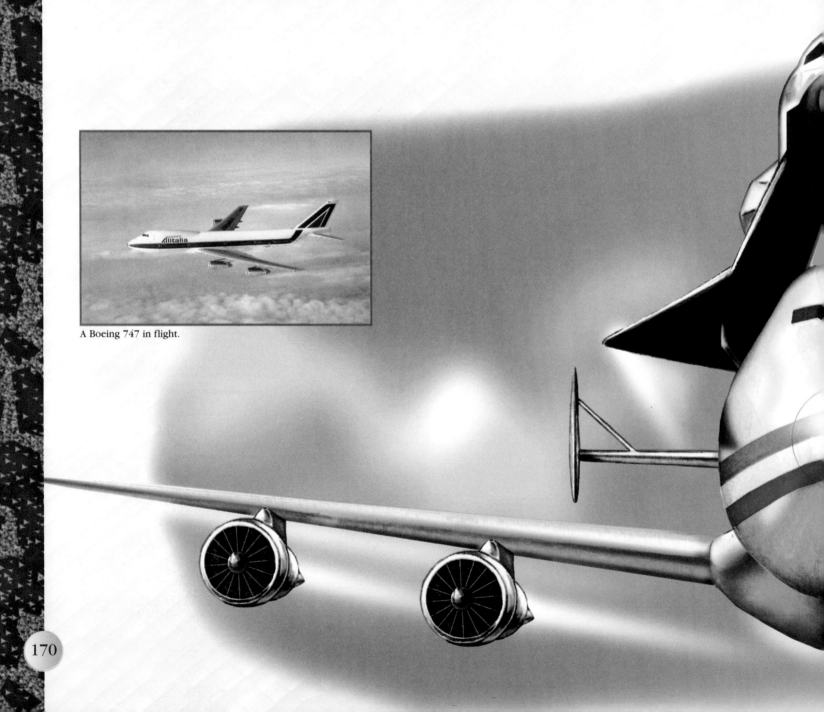

A Boeing 747 in flight.

FACT

The airport at **Bangda** in Tibet is the 'highest' in the world, 4739 above sea level. It also has the longest runways for take-off and landing, at 5500 metres. The international airport of **Schiphol** on the outskirts of Amsterdam, Holland, is 5.5 metres below sea level.

A THOUSAND PASSENGERS FLY

Each year over one billion travellers and tourists go by air to their destinations. The flight company which transports the highest number of passengers is the American **Delta Air Lines** *- 105,534,000 each year, which is equal to half the total population of one of the major cities in the United States. Second is another American airline,* **United Airlines**, *which carries 87,000,000 passengers each year, then* **American Airlines**, *81,000,000.* **British Airways** *is the busiest airline in intercontinental flights, taking about 37,000,000 passengers along scheduled routes to most countries of the world. The busiest intercontinental route is* **London to New York**, *with around 4,000,0000 passengers each year - the same number as those using the busiest local business route between* **Hong Kong** *and* **Taipie** *in Taiwan.*

Head in the clouds...

The fastest aircraft in the world is the **Lockheed SR-71 Blackbird** (photograph, right-hand page), which can fly at a maximum speed of 3529 kilometres an hour - about the same speed as a rocket! At 32.8 metres long and with a wingspan of 17 metres, it has been in service from 1966 to 1990, used mainly by NATO (North Atlantic Treaty Organization) for research purposes. On 1 September 1974, it established a record for a transatlantic crossing with the unbelievable time of 1 hour, 54 minutes and 56 seconds.

The **Concorde** (centre photograph) is the only supersonic passenger aircraft. It completed the same crossing in 3 hours, 50 minutes, almost twice the time of Lockheed! However, the fastest aircraft ever built remains the American **X-15** (centre spread). This was a prototype ('trial' model, only one built) which in 1967, flew at 7279 kilometres per hour, or 'Mach 7' which is equal to seven times the speed of sound. The **Blackbird** holds the record for the first horizontal flight at the highest level - 26,000 metres. Just to compare - a **Boeing 747** travels at a speed of 10,000 metres altitude.

Giants of the air

The *Boeing 747-400*, or Jumbo Jet, is the largest aircraft in the world. It has a wingspan of 65 metres, the fuselage is longer than 70 metres, it weighs over 320 tonnes and can carry 566 passengers. There are about one thousand of this type of aircraft in service. The Russian *Antonov Au-225* is the heaviest, weighing 508 tonnes.

AROUND THE WORLD...IN 31 HOURS!

*The fastest round-the-world flight was established by an Air France **Concorde**. It left New York on 15 August 1995 travelling east. The flight was completed in 31 hours, 27 minutes and 49 seconds, with landings for refuelling at Tolosa, Dubai, Bangkok, Guam, Honolulu and Acapulco.*

FACT

The Russian Mil Mi-26 is the largest *helicopter* in the world, capable of lifting a weight of 56,000 kilograms.
It is 40 metres long, with rotor blades 32 metres in diameter. It is used mainly for military purposes, for the transport of special troops.

Earth, air, water, fire

The largest fire-fighting aircraft is the Russian-built **Ilyushin 76 TD**. It can transport up to 42,000 litres of water. On each journey, it can pour its cargo over an area 1200 metres wide and 90 metres long, extinguishing in a short time the most extensive blaze.

The heaviest hydroplane is the **Martin XP6M-1 Seamaster**, an aircraft designed by the United States Navy. Four reactor motors give it the power to exceed speeds of 1000 kilometres per hour.

FACT

In 1986, American pilots Dick Rutan and Jeanna Yeager made the first flight around the world in an aircraft without stops or refuelling, flying in an 'ultra-light' aircraft called **Voyager**, in a time of 9 days, 3 minutes and 44 seconds.

Hydroplane

A HUGE AIRSHIP

The largest-ever airship was a German-built **Zeppelin** *called Hindenburg. It was 245 metres long (more than three times the size of a Jumbo Jet) and went into regular service on some routes, just like a modern airliner. Then in 1937, after just one year in service, it burst into flames on take-off (see picture). 35 people were killed.*

THE 'ELDER STATESMAN' OF THE SKIES

The firm which has produced the most aircraft in the world is the **Cessna Aircraft Company** *of Wichita, Kansas, USA. This company has made more than 183,000 aircraft since 1911.*

Railway and trains

The **United States** can boast the longest railway network in the world - 234,000 km., carrying an estimated 20,300 locomotives and 3 million trucks. 'Second place' goes to **Russia**, with 154,000 km., followed by **Canada** (73,000), **China** (67,500), **India** (60,000) and **Germany** (37,500). The **United States**, **China** and **Russia** use their railways more for the transport of goods. **Japan** and **Switzerland** concentrate on the requirements of the high number of passengers who use the trains for travelling around. The longest railway in the world, over 10,000 km. long is the **Trans Siberian** railway. It was completed in 1905 and covers a vast length of the country, equal to almost a quarter of the circumference of the globe. It takes eight days to travel along the railway from Moscow, Russia's capital city, to the port of Vladivostok in Siberia.

The longest **straight railway**, an uninterrupted stretch of rails disappearing on the horizon, goes across 478 km. of the Australian Nullarbar plain, without a single curve or obstacle on the way.

French TGV

The highest railway in the world in the Andes

FACT

The **highest railway** in the world climbs the Peruvian Andes to a height of 4817 metres, higher than the summit of Mont Blanc. Just imagine the breathtaking view at the end of the journey!

Canadian Railways train

View of the Trans Siberian railway

HARES AND SNAILS ON WHEELS

Australia *holds the record for the longest and heaviest train in the world. The convoy, composed of 682 wagons loaded with steel minerals, and pulled by 8 locomotives, takes up 7.3 km. of track, weighs over 100,000 tonnes and connects the mining areas of Yandi and Newman at Port Hedland in Eastern Australia. Nicknamed 'the mole', this train is also very slow. To cover 275 kilometres, it takes at least ten hours, far longer than a racing cyclist would take to complete the same distance. The fastest train in the world is the* **Nozomi** *on the Japanese railways, which travels on the line which connects Hiroshima to Kokura, on the island of Honshu, at an average speed of 262 km. per hour, just a little faster than the 256 km. per hour of the French* **TGV***. The TGV Atlantic on the track between Courtalain and Tours has reached a maximum speed of 515 km. per hour... something to challenge the most powerful Formula 1 racing car! On 14 April 1994, a Japanese railways* **Maglev** *train (see centre picture) reached a speed of 552 km. per hour! This train has magnets instead of wheels and runs along a magnetic track. The two magnetic sources constantly repel (push apart), so that the Maglev is suspended slightly above the track as it moves along.*

Ships and ports

The **Japanese** have the largest merchant fleet in the world - over 8000 ships, compared to 6000 registered in **Panama** and 5800 in the **United States**.

Rotterdam in Holland is the largest commercial port. 294 million tonnes of goods pass through its docks each day, compared to 290 million tonnes loaded by container in **Singapore** and 174 million tonnes in **Chiba**, Japan.

The Voyager of the Seas is the largest cruise ship in the world. With a tonnage of 142,000 tonnes, this giant of the seas can transport 3840 passengers and over 1181 members of crew. It is as long as three American football pitches, and has a theatre, golf course, ice-skating rink, ballroom, gyms, three swimming pools each with sauna, 3 restaurants, 14 lifts and more than 3000 cabins.

Cruise Liner

An icebreaker ship

SAILS UNFURLED

The largest sailing ship in the world is the **Royal Clipper**. *Its five wooden masts rise up as high as a 15-floor building. Fully unfurled, its 42 sails catch the wind with all their 5202 square metres of material. At 134 metres long and with a weight of 5000 tonnes, it can carry 228 passengers and 106 members of crew. On board there are 3 swimming pools, a gymnasium with central heating, elegant shops and a large dining room, from which diners can admire the sunset on the Caribbean sea...*

FACT

The 'Monster of the Caspian Sea' was the largest **hydrofoil** ever built. With a weight of 514 tonnes, it looked rather like a cross between an aeroplane and a hovercraft, travelling on the surface of the water at a speed approaching 500 kilometres an hour, powered by 10 turbines. It was completely destroyed in 1980 and has not been replaced.

The port of Singapore

TOP SPEED ACROSS THE WAVES

The speed record for a boat was established in October 1978 by the **Spirit of Australia** *(see centre spread). This was a hydroplane equipped with a J34 Westinghouse jet engine which made it more like a 'flying boat'. Over a distance of around one kilometre in the Blowering Dam Lake in New South Wales, Australia it reached a speed of 514.36 kilometres per hour.*

Giants of the sea

The largest **aircraft carriers** in the world are those which belong to the class **Nimitz**, in the service of the United States Navy. Each one is more than 300 metres long, with a weight of 98,500 tonnes and equipped with a runway of 18,200 square metres, on which aircraft can take off every 20 seconds. The Nimitz can sail at a speed of 30 knots (about 60 km. per hour) thanks to four nuclear turbines which supply a power of 260,000-horse power.

The largest **petrol tanker** which sails the seas is the **Leviathan**, which can transport up to 250,000 tonnes of crude oil.

The **goods freighter** with the largest capacity is the **Jahre Viking**, which, when fully loaded, sails with 300,000 tonnes of goods destined for ports all around the world.

FACT

The largest **hovercraft** in the world is the **SR.N4 MKIII**. It is 56 metres long and weighs 310 tonnes. The USA military hovercraft, **SES-100B** holds the speed record for travelling on the surface of the sea at 170 km. per hour.

HEAVYWEIGHTS!

The **Rossiya**, launched in the shipyards of Saint Petersburgh in Russia is the largest ice-breaking ship in the world. It weighs 23,500 tonnes and has a nuclear propulsion of 75,000-horse power. The largest river boat is the **Mississippi Queen**, a steam-driven sailing ship 116 metres long and famous for its characteristic paddle wheel. It is still in service on the Mississippi River in the United States (photograph, left-hand page).

Submarines

The fastest submarines in the world are the nuclear powered submarines in the class **Alpha**, in service with the Russian Navy. These submarines can go at an average speed of 40 knots (about 75 km. per hour). They also hold the record for the highest number of dives on active service - more than 120, diving to a depth of 760 metres. Like American-built submarines, the **Alpha** class is able to cover a distance of 640,000 kilometres, equal to 15 times around the world, without having to refuel.

THE 'GNOME' OF THE SEA

The **coracle** is the smallest **boat** in the world. It is shaped rather like a walnut shell with just enough room for one person and a paddle (see small picture). Coracles are still used by fishermen in Ireland, Wales and France. The **sailing boat** is faster and also the **windsurf** which skims across the water at 80 km. an hour! This speed was beaten by the trimaran **Yellow Pages Endeavour** on 26 October 1993. At Sandy Point near Melbourne, Australia it reached a speed of 46.52 knots - over 86 km. per hour.

ALONE IN THE OCEAN

The first round-the-world non-stop **solo** voyage in a yacht was achieved by British yachtsman Robin Knox-Johnston on board the Suhaili. The voyage lasted from 14 June 1968 until 22 April 1969 - over 312 days of non-stop navigation, with only the wind and the waves for company.

Trams and the underground

The Docklands Light Railway, London

The **London Underground** is the oldest underground system. The first line was opened to the public in 1863. It is also the longest and most extensive in the world, with 388 km. of track. Second longest is the **New York Subway**, with 370 km. of track. New York boasts the highest number of stations, 468, and the highest average number of kilometres covered each day - 1.6 million. The **Tokyo** underground is 198 km. long, **Paris Metro** 192 km., whilst **Milan**, the largest underground system in Italy, is only 47 km. long! The highest number of passengers is in **Moscow**, with over 3 billion users per year, against over 2 billion in **Tokyo**, and 1.5 billion passengers on the underground in **Mexico City**. The most extensive tram network in the world is in **Saint Petersburgh** in Russia, which has 2402 trams working on 64 lines which cover a combined length of 690 kilometres.
The oldest train **carriages** still in service are the N.1 and N.2 on the Manx Electric Railways,

regularly used since 1893 along the 28.5 kilometres between Douglas and Ramsey on the **Isle of Man** in the UK.
The largest **bus station** in the world, with room for about 18,400 vehicles, belongs to the transport company in the state of **Andhra Pradesh**, in India.

An old horse-drawn tram on the Isle of Man

ON TWO WHEELS

The fastest model of motorbike in the world is the **Suzuki GSX 1300R Hayabusa**, named after one of the fastest birds in the world, and which can reach speeds of 299 km. per hour. This is followed closely by the **Honda CBR 1100XX**, which reaches 291 km. per hour. In **Holland** there are more bicycles in relation to the population than in any other country in the world - about 16 million, one for each person! In **Japan** and **China** the percentage of cyclists is also high - 2 out of 3 Japanese own a bicycle, and in China there are often three people to be seen travelling on two wheels.

Daedalus

FACT

On 23 April 1988, the Greek Kanellos Kanellopoulos completed the longest flight with a pedal-driven aircraft - a sort of bicycle with streamlined wings, the **Daedalus 88**, which 'took off' from Heraklion, on the island of Crete, towards Santorini (see centre spread). After having pedalled for three hours, 54 minutes and 59 seconds, covering a distance of over 115 km., the progress of the 'aerial bicycle' was suddenly interrupted by a strong gust of wind, and this unusual, daring method of transport landed in the surf on the shore of Santorini.

RECORD NEWS
TRANSPORT

Just around the corner...

According to some of the largest car manufacturers, the car of the future is 'just around the corner'. Perhaps by 2020 or 2030, there will be a car which will drive itself, without the need of a driver. It will be controlled almost completely by technology, powered by non-polluting fuel.

The bodywork will be made of a strong plastic material weighing no more than 500 kg. (less than half the weight of the average car today) and will offer a better resistance against dents and scratches, as well as the rust which affects metal parts.

Windows and lights will be in special ultra-light materials. Ultrasound radar mounted on the bumper will enable the car to avoid collision with other vehicles, as well as selecting a safe cruising speed which will increase or decrease, according to the speed and the presence of other cars, the condition of the road and weather conditions.

Special infra-red tele-cameras will highlight dark images on the road through the windscreen, making driving at night safer and also in the case of fog or bad weather. There will be a special device to stabilize the car if at any time there is a danger of it being overturned and also in the case of the car being abandoned or the driver losing control. Special ecological tyres will enable the car to travel at speeds from 80 km. to 200 km. per hour.

Seats will automatically adapt to the shape of the driver, with exact measurements for the air-bag safety cushion. Seat-belts will adjust to the right tension and tighten up at exactly the right moment a few seconds before any collision.

The gears will be equipped with a system of recognition 'fingerprints' of the owner, whilst an internal tele-camera near the driving seat will observe the driver, giving a warning in the case of temporary lapses of attention or other signs of distraction or tiredness. If, for example, a driver begins to sleep at the wheel, the car will cruise to a stop automatically at the side of the road. A sophisticated computer on board will communicate all information to the driver regarding traffic and driving conditions, regulating the functioning of all the commands and the mechanisms inside the car so that it performs at its best. Also included will be a 'high technology' anti-theft device which can communicate directly with the police station.

So far, there is no information on how the horn and the brakes will work...

INDEX